D0624148

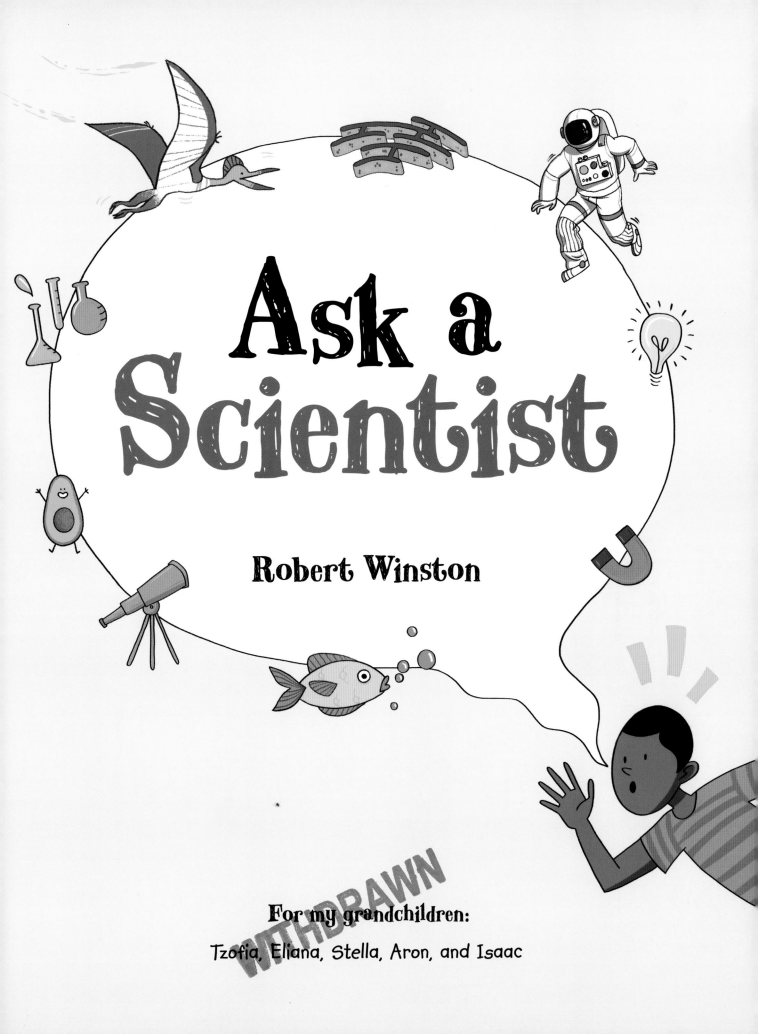

Ask a Scientist

Robert Winston

WITHDRAWN

For my grandchildren:

Tzofia, Eliana, Stella, Aron, and Isaac

Contents

The 100 questions cover these six main science topics, color-coded as follows:

Chemistry

Human body

Physics

Natural science

Earth

Space

In the pages of this book, many answers include words that have been singled out in larger type. This means that the words are expanded upon on the page.

You'll find a glossary at the back of the book that explains any words that you might find tricky to understand.

Foreword

" These are some of the most common questions that you have asked me during my many visits to schools. We also collected questions from children in different parts of the world, including Britain, mainland Europe, the United States, Canada, India, China, and Japan. What is intriguing is that wherever you live, very similar questions crop up everywhere.

This book is my attempt to answer you. Often, many of the wonderful questions you pose are ones that most adults are afraid to ask. I am delighted that you have been ready to ask them. It is important that you are never embarrassed about not knowing something. By asking a question you do what good scientists do. Scientists see something they don't understand and pose a question. Then they consult other scientists and search for any knowledge about the subject they can find. Finally, they plan to find an answer by performing an experiment. Some of your questions in this book are ones I couldn't answer. So I looked stuff up and sometimes consulted other scientists. While I have performed only a few of the experiments myself, the answers I give often depend on experiments done by other scientists.

And just occasionally there's a question that nobody can answer yet. This is why science is so exciting. Because if you become a scientist, you may find answers to things that are still unknown. **"**

Robert Winston.

Why is science so important?

❝ You're reading this book, made by the science of printing. Hopefully you are not shivering with cold, hungry, and in darkness. When you're bored with what I've written, you can watch TV, use a computer, or take a journey on a bus to see your friends. You all are likely to live longer, healthier lives than any previous humans. Science dominates our world, yet we take it for granted. It can also be misused and harm us or our precious planet. So it is really important that each of us understands science better so that we can make wise decisions about how best to use this powerful knowledge. **❞**

What makes someone a scientist?

"People become scientists for many different reasons. When I was 8, I wanted to learn how things worked and tried experiments, which mostly failed. This could be frustrating but was also fun. When I was older, I saw the exquisite beauty of plant and animal tissues through a microscope. At 14 I made a telescope and saw planets and craters on the moon. When I was 16, I finally made a radio that didn't actually catch fire when I turned it on. In college I saw that science was not just interesting. I learned its value to do immense good in all walks of life."

Can we ever be 100% sure?

"I don't think so. In fact, I think it is better to be unsure, even when you think you have what looks like proof of something. And to my mind, the more science we do, the more we find out about what we don't know. Not being sure is why we do science."

What is my body made of?

"Your body is made of about 37 trillion (or 37,000,000,000,000) tiny **cells**. There are about 200 different cell types, which make muscle, nerves, brain, fat, glands, blood, liver, skin, and so on. However, it is even more complicated—your skin has its own cells that make hair, and others that make color for your hair. Some make sweat, and others help you tan in the sun. You have even more bacteria cells in and on your body—about 40 trillion of them. Most bacteria actually keep us healthy, but they are also the main reason why we smell a little bad if we don't wash."

Protein is stored here until it's needed by the cell.

Nerve cells carry messages throughout your body.

Messages travel as electrical signals.

Cells

Inside a cell there are different structures, each with a particular job to do to keep the cell healthy and functioning normally. The cell's control center is the nucleus.

Could you create a human being in a laboratory?

The nucleus is the cell's control center. It stores the cell's DNA.

These rough tubes make proteins.

This produces energy to power the cell.

These are small storage bags that contain nutrients and waste.

These clean up the cell, getting rid of waste and invaders such as germs.

These smooth tubes make and store fats.

66 We can't make a human in a lab because cells cannot be made artificially. If we could make a basic cell, we might be able to turn it into a human egg cell or even a sperm cell. Then we could create a human **embryo**. This is not possible at the moment, but it might be in the distant future. 99

Embryo

An embryo may develop to become a baby in the womb. By the end of eight weeks, all of its bodily organs have begun to form.

Human embryo

When did time begin?

Some ancient Greek **philosophers** believed that the universe had existed forever. Today, scientists think the universe started about 14 billion years ago with the **big bang**. This was presumably when time began. Since then, the universe seems to have been expanding from a tiny point. Before the big bang, time and the laws of physics did not exist. At some time in the future, the universe may start to contract, so it's possible it will eventually end. But be sure to treat people really nicely, just in case time stops in the next week. 99

Big bang

The universe was born in a huge explosion. It took 380,000 years for the first atoms to form, and 180 million years for the first stars to shine.

Philosophers

In the sixth century BCE, Greek philosophers began to question the world around them. Using logic and reason, they tried to understand what they saw.

Why is there no air in space?

" Space is a near vacuum with virtually no matter, including air, in it. The mixture of gases (mostly nitrogen and oxygen) that we call air is held close to the Earth's surface by gravity. As we go upward from the Earth, gravity decreases, and the air gets thinner. At about 62 miles (100 km) above our planet, we reach space. "

What is dark matter doing in space?

" Scientists believe that everything we see in space—planets, stars, and galaxies—is only a tiny part of all the matter that exists in the universe. The rest is invisible **dark matter.** We think dark matter exists because stars and galaxies move faster than we'd expect, so there must be unseen matter exerting a gravitational pull on them. "

Find out more about black holes on page 109.

Dark matter

We cannot see dark matter. However, we think it is spread unevenly through space, and clusters of it apply a gravitational force on stars and galaxies.

Most of what we think of as space is actually dark matter.

How was the first person born?

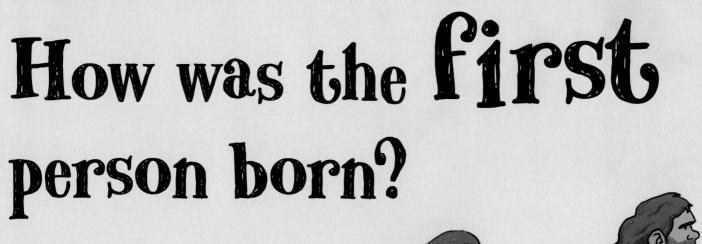

This apelike forest dweller climbed trees, but it could also walk on two legs.

Australopithecus afarensis held its body fairly upright when it walked.

Homo erectus could run and used sharp stones as cutting tools.

Ardipithecus ramidus

Australopithecus afarensis

Homo erectus

66 Scientifically speaking, there could be no 'first person.' This is because of **evolution**—a very slow, gradual process by which human beings came about and which took place in many parts of the world at the same time. Another thing to mention is that just as **mammals** in the wild deliver and breastfeed their young without assistance from others, early humans would have given birth mostly without help. **99**

This species had a strong, muscular body and a large brain.

Homo heidelbergensis hunted large animals using stone-tipped spears.

Homo heidelbergensis

Homo sapiens

Evolution

The first humans appeared in Africa between 8 and 6 million years ago. Since then, there have been many human species, but all are now extinct except for *Homo sapiens*.

Modern humans have less body hair, longer legs, and shorter arms than their extinct, apelike relatives.

We think *Homo sapiens* has been on Earth for 100,000 years. Each new generation takes about 20 years to produce children, so there have been only about 5,000 generations since humankind began!

Mammals

Mammals are animals with backbones and body hair, and they feed their babies milk. Almost all mammals give birth to live young, except for platypuses and echidnas, which lay eggs. Young mammals stay with their mothers until they can find their own food.

Polar bear cubs stay with their moms for 30 months.

Female chimps usually have one baby at a time.

A mother pig may suckle 10 piglets at once!

Human babies learn to crawl at 6–10 months.

Why does water feel wet?

Strictly speaking, water isn't 'wet.' If you stick your finger in a glass of water, it does not feel wet. However, pull it out of the water, and your finger is wet and feels wet. Wetness is the ability of a fluid to stick to the surface of a solid. Pure water is quite wet, but it sticks to surfaces more if it's mixed with soap—when it becomes 'wetter.' This is because the forces that bind the **water molecules** to each other are loosened, and this reduces the water's **surface tension**.

Surface tension

Forces that hold liquid molecules together make the surface of a liquid behave like a stretched, elastic skin. This is called surface tension.

Surface tension pulls water into droplets, and gravity pulls the droplets down into teardrop shapes.

Surface tension allows some insects to walk on water.

Water molecules are packed together closely.

Water molecules

Each water molecule is made of three tiny particles called atoms, two of which are hydrogen, and one of which is oxygen. That's why water has the formula H_2O.

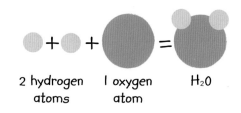

2 hydrogen atoms   1 oxygen atom H_2O

Why are there bubbles in boiling water?

Find out more about bubbles on pages 114–115.

66 Water has some air dissolved in it. As the water is heated, the air is no longer dissolved and forms bubbles that rise to the surface. Once the water is boiling, the bubbles are not filled with air but with water vapor, or steam. At 212°F (100°C), water ceases to be a liquid and forms a gas, so these bubbles are the gaseous form of water—steam. 99

Why doesn't oil mix with water?

66 Oil is less dense (lighter) than water, so it floats on top of the water. Water molecules bind so closely to each other that water does not readily mix with oil, unless you introduce something like soap that loosens the water molecules. 99

Dish soap lifts oil and grease off dirty dishes.

The simple answer to this is no. This is because of something called **gravity**, which is an invisible force that pulls objects together and keeps us on Earth. All objects attract, or pull on, each other with gravity, and very large objects, such as stars and planets, have greater **mass** and therefore apply more force. Jupiter, for example, is the solar system's largest planet and has almost 2.5 times as much gravity as Earth.

Could you jump off the world?

Gravity

Born in 1643, English scientist Isaac Newton was one of the first people to study gravity. There's a story that while he sat under an apple tree, an apple fell from it and hit his head. Newton asked himself why the apple didn't fall up into the sky. He formed a theory that the force of Earth's gravity pulls all objects toward the center of the planet.

Why is there less gravity on the moon?

> " The strength of the pull of gravity depends on the size of the object. Earth is larger than the moon, with more **mass**, so the pull of gravity on Earth is stronger than it is on the moon. This is why astronauts can jump higher and more easily on the moon. "

Find out more about gravity on pages 78–79.

Mass

The mass of an object is the amount of stuff, or matter, that it contains. The more matter there is inside it, the greater the object's mass. Weight is the amount of force acting on an object.

Jupiter vs Earth
Let's say you weigh around 66 lb (30 kg) on Earth. If you were standing on Jupiter, you would weigh about 160 lb (72 kg)—that's about the weight of an adult male.

Moon vs Earth
If you were on the moon, you would weigh just under 11 lb (5 kg), about the same as a cat. This is because gravity is about one-sixth of what it is on Earth, since the moon is smaller with less mass.

Why is the sky blue?

66 Although the light from the sun looks white, it's actually made up of all the colors of the rainbow. Light travels in waves, and each color of light has its own wavelength—some colors have short waves, while others have long waves. When sunlight reaches Earth's atmosphere, it hits gas molecules and floating dust particles. This scatters the different colors. More short-wave blue light is scattered toward our eyes than colors with longer wavelengths, making the sky seem blue. Violet has an even shorter wavelength, so you'd expect the sky to look violet. However, human eyes are more sensitive to blue than violet, so we see a blue sky, not a violet one. 99

Wavelength

Colors at the red end of the light spectrum have longer waves than those at the violet end.

Red

Orange

Yellow

Green

Light blue

Blue

Violet

Rainbow

You see a rainbow when the sun is behind you and it's raining in front of you. As white sunlight shines through millions of raindrops, it splits into an arc of different colors.

Light is bent, or refracted, as it passes into and out of the raindrop.

Each wavelength is refracted at a different angle.

The light spreads out into a spectrum.

Why do I see different colors in the sky at sunset?

❝ As the sun sinks in the sky to the horizon, it has to shine through much more of Earth's atmosphere and therefore travels through more particles and dust. The blue light gets scattered even more, and then the longer wavelength light—like red and yellow—becomes more visible. ❞

Will scientists bring back the dinosaurs?

Borealopelta markmitchelli was discovered in 2011 in Alberta, Canada. It is one of the world's best-preserved dinosaur fossils.

Find out more about dinosaurs on pages 74–75.

" A few scientists have tried, but I think there's little chance of success. They hope to retrieve **dinosaur DNA** from blood or a skeleton, or possibly from a biting insect such as a **mosquito**. The problem is that DNA breaks down as it ages. So far, nobody has retrieved intact DNA strands from more than about one million years ago—long after dinosaurs died out. "

Dinosaur DNA

To re-create a dinosaur, scientists would need its complete DNA, not just pieces of it. Because dinosaurs became extinct over 60 million years ago, this is unlikely to be found. You'd also need a dino mom to incubate, or look after, the egg.

Mosquito

This ancient mosquito is trapped in amber—fossilized tree sap. Its body may contain the DNA of dinosaurs whose blood it sucked millions of years ago.

Is it possible to find a fossil that no one has discovered yet?

" Yes! In August 2018, scientists found a previously unknown worm that lived more than 400 million years ago in Britain. New fossils are discovered each week, and **new species** are often identified. So far, around 1,000 different types of dinosaur have been found, but we've probably dug up only a small fraction of all the species that existed. **"**

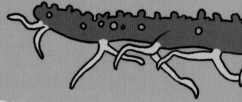

New species

The new species of worm was found in 430-million-year-old rocks in Britain. Called *Thanahita distos*, it was a wormlike creature with legs.

Jurassic Coast cliffs at West Bay in Dorset

On vacation in Dorset, England, I was just 12 when I found a fossil trilobite, a common sea species that was a little like a very large centipede. It lived about 200 million years ago.

Trilobite

Where does my belly button go?

Innies and outies

After the umbilical cord has been cut, the stub of the cord falls off. This leaves a scar, which is what your belly button really is. People with "outies" just have a little bit more scar tissue than people with "innies."

Outie button

Innie button

❝ It doesn't go anywhere, but it did once! When you were in your mom's **womb**, the only thing that connected you to her was your umbilical cord. This went from your belly button (or umbilicus) to the placenta, an organ attached to the lining of the womb. The cord carried blood from your mom's placenta to your body, providing all the **nutrients** and oxygen you needed to keep you healthy until birth. After you were born, the cord was cut. All that's left is your belly button. **❞**

Placenta
The placenta is your life-support system when you're in the womb.

Womb

The womb, also called the uterus, is the organ in which babies develop. It's a hollow chamber with muscular walls.

Umbilical cord
The umbilical cord is up to 24 in (60 cm) long.

Nutrients

Nutrients are the substances in food that we need for energy and growth. The umbilical cord carries nutrient-rich blood from the mother to her baby.

Why does ice cream melt?

" All matter can exist in one of several states. This depends mostly on temperature. Very cold things turn solid: for example, water becomes ice. As it gets warmer, the molecules in a substance move faster, and it turns to liquid, or melts. When heated more, gas, like steam, is formed. Interestingly, when you put any gas under high pressure, it can become liquid again, even though it is still hot. Different substances become **solids, liquids,** and **gases** at varying temperatures. "

Ice cream is made mostly of water, which melts at 32°F (0°C).

Solids

A solid has a fixed shape. Its molecules can vibrate but can hardly move position.

Liquids

Liquid molecules are farther apart than solid molecules, allowing the liquid to flow.

Gases

Gas molecules are far apart and can move freely, so a gas always spreads out.

Plasma

Plasma often forms when a gas gets so hot that electrons break away from their atoms. That's what happens inside a plasma ball, or lamp.

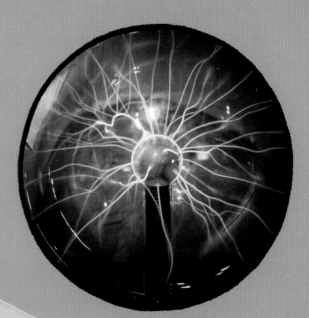

Find out more about molecules on pages 58–59.

66 Fire is none of these states of matter. This is a rather mysterious question, and the answer is also a problem. Fire is actually a chemical reaction that is occurring in a hot gas. The chemical reaction is between oxygen and the substance that's burning. There is a fourth state of matter, called plasma, which is often very hot indeed. In a way, fire is closest to plasma. This forms when atoms start to break up into their different parts. 99

Is fire a solid, liquid, or gas?

How do  maglev trains work?

66 If you've played with magnets, you know that opposite **poles** attract and similar poles repel each other. When an electrical current flows through a wire, it creates an electromagnet. Powerful electromagnets on a maglev train repel other electromagnets on the track. The train 'floats' on this magnetic field and is kept on the track without touching it by metal guides. Magnets also drive it forward, and because the train does not touch the track, it is **frictionless**. This enables it to run fast using less energy. 99

Two south poles (or two north poles) repel—they push away from each other.

Opposite poles (a north and a south) attract—they pull toward each other.

Poles

The two ends of a magnet are called poles. The gray iron filings on these magnets show what can happen when two poles meet.

Frictionless

Friction is a force that slows down moving things by pulling against the direction of the movement. Smooth surfaces slipping past each other create less friction or are frictionless.

Skates gliding on ice create an almost frictionless surface.

28

The train's smooth and streamlined shape helps it move through the air at high speeds.

Maglev train in Shanghai, China

How does a maglev train Stop?

"When current flows through them, electromagnets in the track pull and push on magnets in the train, propelling it forward. When **braking**, the current is reversed, so the electromagnets pull and push in the opposite direction."

Braking

A maglev doesn't have brakes with moving parts like a normal train. To slow down and stop, the direction of the magnetic fields is simply reversed.

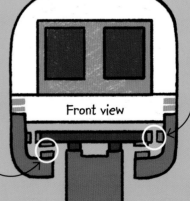

These magnets stop the train from touching the sides of the track.

Front view

These magnets lift the train above the track, move it forward, and slow it down.

When current flows one way, the magnets interact and speed up the train. When current flows the other way, the magnets' fields switch direction and bring the train to a halt.

Does a butterfly remember its time as a caterpillar?

" A butterfly has **four stages** of development—egg, caterpillar (larva), chrysalis (pupa), and adult. I doubt if it remembers anything from the three early stages! **"**

Four stages

4. Adult
The winged adult emerges from the chrysalis.

1. Egg
Adult females lay tiny eggs on plants.

2. Caterpillar
The caterpillar hatches and spends its time feeding.

3. Chrysalis
Inside a silk cocoon, the caterpillar's body changes.

How do butterflies sleep?

" Butterflies don't actually sleep. Instead, they rest at night, or in the day when there's little sunlight, or if it is cool, raining, or cloudy. Sometimes they rest hidden among leaves or while hanging upside down from branches. **"**

Butterflies rest and wait for warm, dry weather.

Spider silk is made of protein. It's incredibly stretchy and is one of the strongest of all natural materials.

Sticky silk traps insects.

Silk emerges from openings on the spider's abdomen.

The spider's web is often a geometric pattern, with the strands laid out at regular intervals.

The spider wraps its prey before eating it.

How do spiders make webs?

❝ Not all spiders make webs, but many species make **silk** from multiple tiny glands in the tips of their abdomens. Each of these glands can make a different type of silk—silk that builds the basic web, sticky silk for catching insects, and fine silk for wrapping up captured prey. Spiders often start a web with a long 'trailing' silk that floats in the wind before it sticks to a nearby surface, such as a branch. **❞**

How do we get taller?

> A gland called the **pituitary**, which is attached under the brain, produces **growth hormone**. This circulates in the blood and acts on the liver to produce another hormone called 'growth factor.' These two hormones stimulate muscle, bone, and other tissues to make more cells, so that your body grows.

Giant of a man

On rare occasions, the pituitary gland can work too much. Possibly the tallest man who ever lived was American Robert Wadlow, who grew to an enormous 8 ft 11 in (2.72 m). This was probably because his pituitary gland was extra large and produced too much growth hormone.

Pituitary

Hormones are chemicals made by glands. They're like messengers, traveling in your blood and telling different parts of your body what to do. The pituitary is the main hormone-producing gland.

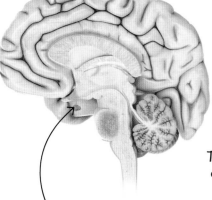

The pituitary is about the size of a pea.

The tiny pituitary, at the base of the brain, makes eight important hormones.

Growth hormone

The pituitary gland releases eight doses of growth hormone every day. The hormone makes your body's cells divide and multiply. Most growth hormone is released at night. Growth hormone levels fall sharply once you're an adult.

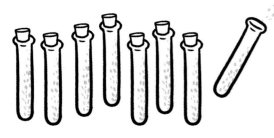

What causes growing pains?

66 Some children get aching legs at night. People often call these aches 'growing pains.' It's not clear what causes the pains, but most doctors think it has nothing to do with growing. Children who are very active or who have very flexible joints seem more likely to have achy legs at night. Unless they have other symptoms as well, it's usually nothing to worry about. 99

How do animals camouflage?

Stick insects look like... sticks!

Leopard

With its spotted coat, the leopard blends in with the background. It is careful not to move or moves very slowly. It is much easier to spot a moving animal than one that stays still.

Chameleon

A chameleon can change its skin color and pattern to camouflage itself or to signal to other chameleons.

"Animals use camouflage to blend in with their surroundings so they can hide from predators or sneak up on prey. Camouflaged animals are colored and patterned to match their surroundings. Toads, for example, are green and brown like the forest floor, while the spots on a **leopard** merge with the shadows of trees and grasses. Some iguanas and tree snakes are green to match leaves, and the white **Arctic hare** is hard to detect in snow. A few animals, like the **chameleon** and the octopus, can change their skin color chemically to match whatever they are sitting on."

Arctic hare

The Arctic hare's fur is snow-white in winter. Its coat turns gray brown in summer, to hide it among plants and rocks.

Staying hidden

It's not just animals that use camouflage. This photographer is wearing camouflage to get closeup shots of wildlife. Soldiers also use camouflage—greens and browns to hide in jungles and forests, or sandy colors when in the desert.

Is there a magnet so STRONG that it will pull us by the iron in our blood?

66 Unlike the iron in a nail, which is **ferromagnetic**, the iron in our **red blood cells** is in a different form and is hardly magnetic at all. Even if you were in the strongest **magnetic field**, you would not feel any pulling. Your brain has billions of nerve fibers that conduct electricity like wires. When electricity flows, it creates a magnetic field around a wire. We have machines that can detect increases in magnetism in a brain when it is working hard. Yet in school, when you're trying to do tough math problems, the magnetic field you produce is so faint that your heads will not stick together. **99**

The steel in a car is pulled by a magnet because it contains iron.

You are not magnetic. You have only about 0.1 oz (3 g) of iron in your body.

Red blood cells

These blood cells get their red color from a protein called hemoglobin, which contains iron. Hemoglobin collects oxygen as red blood cells pass through the lungs.

A junkyard magnet is an electromagnet—it's only magnetic when electricity flows through it.

Red blood cells carry oxygen around the body.

The mineral magnetite is naturally ferromagnetic. It will attract objects containing iron, such as steel pins.

Ferromagnetic

Some metals, such as iron and nickel, become magnetized when put in a magnetic field and stay magnetized even after the field is removed. We say they are ferromagnetic.

Find out more about magnets on pages 28–29.

Magnetic field

Every magnet is surrounded by a magnetic field—a zone in which it can pull on other objects. The pulling force loops around the poles at each end of the magnet.

A magnetic field is invisible, but you can see its effects by sprinkling iron filings around a magnet.

"You may want to use a magnifying glass to look at two attached Velcro® strips. You'll see that one strip has tiny hooks, while the other has little loops. When the strips are pressed together, the hooks grip the loops so that the two sides stick—an example of science and engineering imitating nature. George de Mestral, a Swiss engineer, invented it, eventually selling more than 30,000 miles (50,000 km) of his strips each year."

How does Velcro® stick?

George de Mestral

While out walking in 1941, George de Mestral noticed that his pants and his dog were covered in prickly seedcases called burs. He found that the burs clung to clothes and fur because they were covered in tiny hooks. This gave him the idea for Velcro®—a new way to fasten things.

Velcro®

Remember that if the Velcro® on your sneakers no longer sticks, it's not George de Mestral's fault—your shoes are filthy! Clean the Velcro® with a stiff brush, and it should work again.

The green hooks attach to the blue loops.

Space-age technology

Hook-and-loop fasteners might not seem high tech enough for space missions, but in the 1960s, NASA found that Velcro® was perfect for stopping equipment from floating around in zero gravity. The Apollo astronauts who landed on the moon had Velcro® fasteners on their suits and helmets, too.

How does a **honeybee** know what *job* to do?

66 A fascinating question—scientists at Imperial College, London, where I work, are still trying to find out using powerful microscopes and brain scans. The **bee's brain** is tiny. Yet it can navigate its way across many miles, can remember where it has been, and works with other bees in their different **roles**, building complex structures. **99**

Queen
The queen is the only bee in the hive that lays eggs—up to 2,000 per day!

Worker
Female workers collect nectar and pollen, clean the hive, and look after the queen and the young bees.

Bee's brain

A bee's brain is smaller than a pinhead. Bees can do amazing things with their tiny brains!

Drone
Drones are stingless male bees. Their job is to mate with the queen.

Roles

The different types of *bee* in a hive all have their own jobs to do.

"A bee's **stinger** is like a little hollow needle with barbs attached to it. Once you are stung, it cannot be pulled out by the bee. Sadly, when the bee stings, its stinger and some internal organs are pulled out of its body, and the bee dies. Only honeybees lose their stingers, and only females sting."

When a honeybee stings, the *bulb-shaped* venom sac inside its body pumps melittin into the wound.

Stinger

The stinger injects melittin, the bee's acid venom, which causes the pain and itching after you are stung.

The sharp, slanting barbs stop the stinger from being pulled out of the wound.

Why do bees lose their stingers when they sting?

How do our eyes work so we can see?

Retina

The cells of the retina are sensitive to light, and some can detect color as well.

The image on the retina is upside down. Your brain turns it right side up.

The image from the lens does not pass through air like in a camera but through a watery fluid and onto the retina.

The lens focuses, or brings together, the light rays to form an image on the retina.

Cornea

The clear outer layer, the cornea, is very sensitive. Even when it is touched gently, we shut our eyes immediately. This is to protect the eye from damage.

Optic nerve

A large nerve called the optic nerve connects to the brain.

66 The eye has a lens and **cornea** in the front. At the back is a layer of cells called the **retina**. Light entering the eye passes through the lens onto the retina. As it hits the retina, it produces an electrical signal that travels along the **optic nerve** to the brain to tell us what we are seeing. **99**

Light rays bounce off the object you're looking at and enter your eye.

" Blinking protects the delicate cornea and keeps it moist by spreading a watery fluid across the surface. This also cleans the eye to prevent irritation from dirt. We also blink when we are nervous. Fish don't blink— they don't have eyelids. They show they're nervous in other ways. "

How do **two** eyes make **ONE** picture?

" Each eye sees things slightly differently. The brain merges the information from both eyes, which gives stereoscopic (three-dimensional) vision. This is how we can tell how far away something is. "

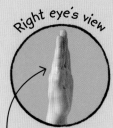

Right eye's view

Try holding your hand in front of you. Look at it with only your right eye open.

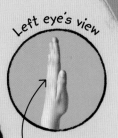

Left eye's view

You can see that the hand looks slightly different with only your left eye open.

43

How do you make gears spin?

The large gear turns more slowly.

Teeth

Here, the large gear has 20 teeth, and the small one has 10. The small gear turns twice as fast, but with half the force. Some gears, like those on a bike, are linked by a chain.

The small gear turns more quickly.

" A gear is a toothed wheel that fits together with other gears. As one gear turns, its **teeth** connect, or mesh, with the second gear's teeth, making the second gear turn in the opposite direction. When the gears are different sizes, they turn at different speeds. A big gear spins a small gear faster, but with less force. A small gear turns a large gear with more force but less speed. "

44

How do elevators work?

❝ Powered by an electric motor, an elevator moves a passenger car up and down using gears, **pulleys**, and cables. Attached to the other end of the cables is a **counterweight**. This moves up when the passenger car descends and moves down when the car rises. Electronic switches start and stop the elevator, and a safety brake prevents the car from falling if the elevator breaks down. ❞

Pulleys

A pulley is a wheel with a rope around it. It makes heavy objects easier to lift by changing the direction of the force. Pulling on the rope at one end lifts something up at the other end.

Electric motor

Pulley

Counterweight

Passenger car

Counterweight

This counterweight balances the weight of the car by moving in the opposite direction of it. This reduces the amount of energy needed to lift the car.

Why do freckles come in **dots** on your face?

Melanin

Melanin is released deep down in the epidermis, the protective layer of the skin, and travels to the surface.

Surface

Epidermis

Find out more about skin on pages 86-87.

> **"** When skin is exposed to the sun, it turns brown. This brown pigment is called **melanin**. The cells in your skin that make it are called melanocytes, and they become active after getting sunlight. People who get a nice tan have melanocytes scattered evenly throughout the skin. However, some people have clusters of melanocytes. These produce melanin unevenly, so after exposure to sun, they get freckles and have to be careful about getting a **sunburn**. It is said that freckles tend to run in families, and certainly there are several **genes** that are likely to be responsible. **"**

Sunburn

If you are freckly, be much more careful in the sun because your skin doesn't have enough melanin to protect you from sunburn. Always wear sunscreen, a hat, and shades.

Genes

Genes are instructions passed on to you from your parents. The color of your skin and eyes, how tall you are, the way you look, and how your body's made are all because of your genes.

Freckles, hair color, and whether your hair is straight or curly are just three characteristics decided by the genes you get from your mom and dad.

Mom  Dad

Olivia

Noah

Jasmine

Olivia's hair is straight and light brown like her dad's, and she also has freckles like him.

Noah's hair is as black and curly as his mom's. He has freckles like his dad.

Jasmine's hair is curly like her mom's. Like her, she has no freckles.

47

As water droplets combine with each other, they become too heavy and fall as rain.

Why doesn't rain taste salty?

Water cycle

Water is constantly moving between the land, rivers, oceans, and the sky. This is called the water cycle.

The rainwater returns to the seas.

Rivers don't get very salty because they are constantly refilled with fresh rainwater.

Morning fog often clears as the sun warms the air.

How is fog made?

66 Fog is a cloud that forms close to the ground. When warm air containing water vapor cools, the drop in temperature causes the vapor to change into tiny water droplets. These hang in the air as fog. 99

" Rain is made from pure water that has evaporated mostly from the sea and formed clouds. When the clouds cool, it causes rainfall. This is part of the **water cycle**. Heat from the sun causes **evaporation** of ocean water, but the salt remains dissolved in the sea. Rainwater doesn't taste salty but may taste different from drinking water because when it falls through our atmosphere, it picks up dust and other particles. "

Sun

Evaporation

When water evaporates, it changes from a liquid to an invisible gas called water vapor. When this turns back into liquid, we say it condenses.

Clouds are made of tiny water droplets that are so small they float in air.

Plants suck up moisture from the ground and release water vapor from their leaves.

Water vapor from the sea cools in the air and condenses into clouds.

Why is the sea salty?

" Salt (sodium chloride) is one of the most common minerals. It is found naturally in rocks, and it easily dissolves in water. When it rains, water dissolves salt from the rocks. The rainwater washes this salt into rivers, which carry it into the sea. "

Salt from sea spray has collected on this beach log.

Do dogs Cry?

66 Biologists think that only humans truly shed **tears**. Dogs don't cry, though their eyes may look watery sometimes, and neither do our closest relatives, apes. However, animals certainly feel and show **emotion**. Rabbits, dogs, and most mammals make all kinds of noises that show distress, anxiety, or sadness. 99

Human emotion

These children are showing their feelings very clearly! A scientist named Dr. Paul Ekman from California said there are six key emotions that humans show in their facial expressions. These are happiness, surprise, sadness, anger, disgust, and fear. People all over the world use similar expressions to show these emotions.

Sad

Surprised

Happy

Angry

A lifetime's worth of tears is enough to have a bath in.

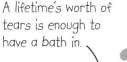

Emotion

Most animals don't show their emotions on their faces like we do. Yet the sounds they make can give us a clue to their feelings. Monkeys might screech and cats hiss to show they're upset or as a warning to stay away.

Screech!

Hiss!

Tears

It's calculated that an average person will shed about 14 gallons (65 liters) of tears during their lifetime—a little more if they grow up with several younger brothers or sisters who constantly annoy them!

How do boogers

66 Boogers are a mixture of dead cells shed from the inside of your nose, partly dried **mucus**, and clumps of tiny living things called bacteria. They get their dark color from the dirt we **breathe** in from the outside air, which is trapped by our nose hair, and they may be green or bluish when we have an **infection** from bacteria that are that color. **99**

Breathe

The last thing your body wants is for dirt to get into your lungs when you breathe. This is why boogers are so important!

Infection

When the body gets infected, we sneeze or cough a lot as a way of getting rid of the mucus that contains the virus. This helps rid the body of the infection.

get in my nose?

Mucus

Mucus is a slimy, sticky fluid that coats the inside of your nose. It may look disgusting, but it has an important job to do. It traps dirt, pollen, and even viruses (tiny things that can cause colds).

Mucus and nose hairs work together to collect dirt and dust. This is where bacteria can form.

Small hairs line the inside of your nose.

Dirt and mucus combine to form boogers!

When we breathe in air through our noses, we also breathe in dust and dirt.

Why will the sun explode and make us extinct?

Sun

The sun is a star. Stars are vast balls of amazingly hot gases, mainly hydrogen and helium, held together by gravity. Stars come in different sizes. They also vary in terms of temperature, color, brightness, and in what they contain.

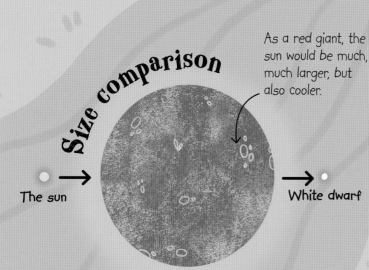

Size comparison

As a red giant, the sun would be much, much larger, but also cooler.

The sun → → White dwarf

Red giant

Red giant

Red giants are small or medium-sized stars that are running out of hydrogen fuel. The surface layers of the star are pushed out due to lack of hydrogen, and the star swells to many times its normal size.

"Only really big stars end their lives with a massive explosion. The good news is that our **sun** is a medium-sized star, so it won't explode! When the sun runs out of fuel, it will probably swell up into a **red giant**. Then it will puff away its outer layers, leaving just a fading, cooler core called a **white dwarf**. Nobody knows exactly when this will happen, but it won't be for billions of years, so we are not likely to become **extinct** before your great, great, great, great, great, great grandchildren leave school!"

Find out more about the sun on pages 88–89.

Extinct

Extinct means to die out completely—forever. The dinosaurs, for example, became extinct about 65 million years ago.

The dinosaurs probably died out when a huge meteorite, or space rock, struck the Earth.

White dwarf

A white dwarf is the last stage in the life of a star like the sun. It is the collapsed core of a red giant. White dwarfs are still hot, and very dense, and they continue to glow faintly for billions of years.

Why don't jellyfish tentacles get tangled?

Tentacles

Jellyfish tentacles drift freely in the current. They sting, grab, and haul in their prey.

❝ Jellyfish rarely get tangled **tentacles.** Even though they don't have brains, they recognize their own cells and don't sting themselves or their own species. Also, they are covered with a protective layer of **MUCUS** that keeps them slippery, which helps. However, occasionally, if they are sick or in water without a steady current, they can get knotted up. I would not like to try to untangle them, would you? **❞**

Mucus

Jellyfish are covered in slimy mucus that helps protect them from infection.

A sick jellyfish that can't untangle itself may break off the knotted tentacles.

" Fish are generally very sensitive to light, so they can see in very **dim light.** Deep below the surface, the water filters out longer wavelengths, leaving only blue light that fish's eyes are particularly adapted to. In very deep water, there is no light at all, and many deep-sea fish are **luminescent**—they make their own light. Most fish are also sensitive to vibration, so they use organs in their sides to detect movement or changes in water pressure. **"**

How do fish see at night?

Dim light

By day, sunlight doesn't penetrate water deeper than 660 ft (200 m). The moon and stars illuminate surface waters a little at night.

This toothy angler uses a glowing lure to attract prey in the darkness.

Luminescent

Some deep-sea fish make light using special chemicals, while others have light-producing bacteria living in their bodies.

How do the molecules in air produce air pressure?

❝ Air pressure is the weight of the **atmosphere** pressing on you. The gas molecules that make up air (mainly nitrogen and oxygen) may *be* incredibly small, but because each one has a tiny amount of mass, Earth's gravity *still* gives them weight. The combined weight of the huge numbers of molecules in the atmosphere presses down on everything *below*—including us. Air pressure is greatest at ground level, since there is a large weight of air overhead. The higher you go, the less air there is above you, so the less pressure there is. **❞**

On a mountaintop, the air molecules are more spaced out, so the air pressure is lower. The air is thinner so we feel the need to breathe faster to get enough oxygen.

Atmosphere

The air molecules in the atmosphere are constantly on the move, bouncing off each other and everything around them.

Air molecules are closely packed at ground level, so the air pressure is greater.

How many atoms are in a penny?

66 Let's do the math! A penny weighs about 0.09 oz (2.5 g). It is made out of two metals, zinc and copper. It has 2.24×10^{22} zinc **atoms** and 5.92×10^{20} copper atoms. That means a penny has a total of 200,000,000,000,000,000,000,000 atoms. I admit this amount is only approximate, because it took me quite a long time to count them all, and, because they are so small, I may have counted some atoms twice! **99**

Find out more about atoms on page 105.

Atoms

Atoms are the *building blocks* of everything in the universe. Inside an atom, electrons whiz around the atom's core, or nucleus.

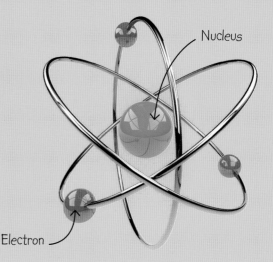

Nucleus

Electron

Why does chocolate taste so good?

" Chocolate is a high-energy food. It contains stimulants, which act on our brains and make us feel good. About 100,000 years ago, early humans were very vulnerable out on the African plains. They were slow animals with weak teeth and very bad claws. Food was scarce, so they ate food that would give them energy to fuel their bodies until the next time they could eat. Today, we still crave high-energy foods, like chocolate, even though we don't really need them. "

High-energy

We get energy from these three major groups: proteins, fats, and carbohydrates. All three are found in chocolate.

Sugar is a type of carbohydrate. Cacao beans also contain carbohydrates.

Milk is high in protein and is often added to chocolate.

Cocoa butter is a kind of fat.

Chocolate

Chocolate is made from the beans, or seeds, of the cacao plant. After harvesting, the beans are processed to make two ingredients: chocolate liquor and cocoa butter, which are then blended to make chocolate.

Cacao bean

Find out more about taste buds on page 95.

Early humans

Weapons helped early humans catch animals more easily and take down larger prey.

Over time, early humans learned survival skills. They were able to get more food to eat, and this helped them become smarter. Eventually, they became the species we are today, Homo sapiens.

They threw wooden spears tipped with sharpened flints to bring down animals.

When electricity travels through wires, what does it look like?

" Electricity is the passage of electrons—tiny parts of an atom that are too small to be seen. You can, however, see the effects of electricity. If a strong electric current is passed through thin, uncovered wire, it meets resistance, and the wire may heat up. If the wire gets very hot, it starts to glow and becomes red or white hot. **Sparks** also show electricity in action. **"**

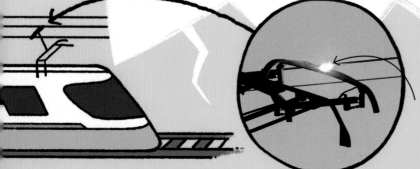

Sparks may fly when trains pick up electricity from overhead cables.

Sparks

Sparks are like mini lightning bolts. Strong electricity acts on tiny molecules in the air, causing it to glow.

How does electricity get in your body to shock someone?

" When we rub against objects, such as our clothes, electrons can move from the objects and onto us. This builds up a charge of static electricity. Human bodies are good **conductors**, meaning that electricity flows easily through us. So if we touch someone else, this charge may leap across to them as a tiny **electric current**, giving a mini shock. Never play with electricity, because a sudden severe shock can burn your skin or even stop your heart. **"**

The shock when we touch someone else makes us jump, but it's not painful.

Conductors

Good

Our bodies contain lots of salty water, which conducts electricity well. Most metals are also good conductors.

Bad

Materials that don't conduct electricity, such as rubber, are called insulators.

Electric current

A current is a stream of moving electrons. When you connect a lightbulb to a battery, a current flows through a wire to the bulb and lights it up.

Lactic acid

Lactic acid causes the burning we feel when we work our muscles extra hard. This painful sensation gets us to slow down or stop exercising altogether, to prevent muscle damage and allow the body to recover.

On a long bike ride, lactic acid can build up in a cyclist's legs.

66 During exercise, glucose combines with oxygen, producing energy to drive our muscles. As the muscles heat up, all oxygen in the blood supplied to our muscles is used up, and the glucose breaks down into lactic acid. This may be the cause of pain during exercise, but soreness afterward is probably caused by something else. If you think this is complicated, so do scientists! **99**

Why do my muscles hurt when I exercise?

Why does my brother smell when he exercises?

" The stench is made by **bacteria** that feed on your brother's sweat. Depending on his age, your brother may have more than 40 trillion bacteria cells living inside or on his body. After childhood, the bacteria on the skin increase, and many of them love wet, hidden places like a teenager's armpits or feet. Try to get your brother to use soap when he showers. If he won't, chase him into the yard after he exercises and hose him down. "

Bacteria

Bacteria are microscopic living things, each made up of just a single cell. Some bacteria are harmful, but the ones on our skin and in our breathing passages and guts actually help us stay healthy.

"Yes, there are a few. One named **Palaeeudyptes** lived about 40 million years ago. Also called the colossus penguin, this huge bird was about 5 ft 3 in (1.6 m) tall and weighed around 254 lb (115 kg). Palaeeudyptes was discovered in 2014 by Argentinian scientists working in Antarctica. **Anthropornis** was another extinct Antarctic giant. Carolina Acosta, who studied fossils in the region, says this was 'a wonderful time for penguins, when 10 to 14 species lived together along the Antarctic coast.'"

Is there an extinct

4 ft 3 in
(1.3 m)

4 ft
(1.2 m)

Southern birds

Today, penguins are found only in the southern hemisphere. The largest species is the emperor penguin, which lives in Antarctica.

2 ft
(0.6 m)

Even the biggest adult emperor penguins weigh less than half as much as Palaeeudyptes did.

species of penguin?

Palaeeudyptes

Scientists think Palaeeudyptes could have stayed underwater for 40 minutes when diving for fish—15 minutes longer than today's record holder, the emperor penguin.

Anthropornis

Before Palaeeudyptes was discovered, the largest extinct penguin known was Anthropornis. It was a little shorter than Palaeeudyptes and weighed nearly 183 lb (83 kg).

5 ft 3 in
(1.6 m)

How does a light light up?

*When electricity moves through the wire inside a lightbulb, the wire gets hot and glows. This is because the wire, called a filament, is very thin and resists the flow of electric current, changing electrical energy into heat and light. The filament is usually made of a metal called **tungsten**, which melts at very high temperatures. To prevent the filament from burning up, all the oxygen is removed from the bulb. The oxygen is replaced with an inert gas (one that does not react). Some bulbs are filled with **halogen** gas, such as iodine or bromine.*

LED lamps

Light-emitting diodes (LEDs) make light by passing electricity through a material called a semiconductor. Lamps that use LEDs are more efficient than other types of bulb—they last much longer, and they use less power. This is because very little energy is lost as heat.

The inert gas in a bulb is often nitrogen or argon.

Tungsten filament

Insulated light fitting

The inert gas in this bulb is halogen.

Tungsten filament

Tungsten

The tungsten filament is very thin and fragile. If a bulb is dropped on the floor, the bulb may not crack, but the filament can easily break.

Halogen

Using halogen gas in the bulb helps protect the filament. Halogen bulbs last about twice as long as other types of bulbs.

Chemicals usually don't explode when mixed. Try adding table salt (sodium chloride) to vinegar (acetic acid)— nothing much happens, and it doesn't even taste good! For an explosion to happen, there has to be a fierce reaction between the chemicals. Energy is released, usually as heat, and gases form from previously solid or liquid molecules. When gases are produced and heated, they expand rapidly, and this causes an explosion.

Why do chemicals explode

Fierce reaction

A reaction is when two or more things are put together, causing a chemical change. Soda gets its bubbles from carbon dioxide dissolved in the drink. Popping mints into diet soda makes bubbles form quicker than in normal soda—so quickly that the diet soda gushes from the bottle!

A foaming fountain of diet soda and gas bubbles erupts from the bottle.

when mixed together?

3. Bang
The gunpowder in the main chamber explodes. The colorful sparkles are made by burning chemicals called metal salts.

2. Whoosh
As the fuse ignites a small amount of gunpowder, hot gases launch the rocket into the sky.

1. Fizz
Once lit, the fizzing fuse provides the heat to start the reaction.

Find out how volcanoes explode on pages 102–103.

Gas, but no explosion!
The yeast you add to bread dough breaks down starch in the flour, releasing bubbles of carbon dioxide gas. The bubbles make the dough rise before baking. Luckily it's a slow reaction—otherwise baking would be a risky business!

Expand rapidly

Fireworks contain gunpowder. When lit, gunpowder reacts with oxygen in the air to produce hot gases that spread out, or expand, quickly and create an explosion.

How many galaxies are there?

66 The Hubble Space Telescope spent a long time photographing a tiny patch of the sky, collecting faint light from the edge of the visible universe. It found 10,000 **galaxies** in that small area. From Hubble's observations, astronomers estimated that there were 100 to 220 billion galaxies across the whole sky. New research suggests there are more galaxies in the universe that we can't detect with our telescopes, and that the real total is around 2 trillion (2 million million). **99**

Galaxies

A galaxy is a huge group of stars held together by gravity. The biggest galaxy, IC 1101, is about 50–60 times bigger than our galaxy, the Milky Way.

Hubble Space Telescope

Orbiting above Earth's atmosphere, Hubble can take much clearer photographs than telescopes on the ground.

How old is the solar system?

66 Judging from the age of rocks in meteorites, scientists think that the **solar system** is roughly 4.6 billion years old. 99

Solar system

The solar system's eight planets are made of material that was left over after the sun formed.

The sun

Mercury

Jupiter

Earth

Venus

Saturn

Mars

Uranus

Neptune

Does Earth shrink, expand, or remain the same over time?

66 We think that Earth stays roughly the same size. Measurements of Earth's radius suggest that at the moment it's growing by a tiny amount—around 0.004 in (0.1 mm) a year. 99

73

" Strictly speaking, most dinosaurs didn't have wings, but some of their close reptile relatives did. The most famous dinosaur-like creature was Pterodactylus, whose wings measured about 3.5 ft (1 m) from tip to tip. However, a winged lizard called Quetzalcoatlus was even more

Did dinosaurs have wings?

Quetzalcoatlus was covered in feathers.

Quetzalcoatlus

This gargantuan reptile lived around 70 million years ago and snacked on small dinosaurs!

impressive. It had a wingspan of 50 ft (15 m)—that's a little longer than a city bus. It had a massive beak, and it must have needed a lot of energy just to take off. Quetzalcoatlus cruised by soaring, and scientists think it had a top speed of more than 50 mph (80 kph). **99**

Pterodactylus's wings were long and powerful.

Pterodactylus

This reptile had an extra-long fourth finger that supported each wing. Its name means "winged finger."

A nine-year-old child would have been dwarfed by the huge Quetzalcoatlus.

Birds

Did you know some relatives of dinosaurs still exist today? They're called birds! They are the living descendants of small, feathered dinosaurs.

Why do we need a brain?

Movement

Planning movements

Touch

Awareness of space

Thinking and personality

Emotional understanding

Making images

Hearing

Speech

Front of brain

Memory

Seeing

Coordination

The brain is roughly divided into areas that carry out specialized functions.

66 Your brain helps you read this book—to see, think, imagine, figure things out, and remember. It controls **functions** like your heartbeat and breathing. Your brain also helps you feel warmth, pain, and touch, and emotions like sadness, happiness, and anger. Yet not all animals need brains—some **sea creatures** are able to live without them. **99**

Functions

Complex functions such as thinking, memory, speaking, and movements are controlled by the cortex—the brain's wrinkly outer layer.

Sea creatures

A tunicate, or sea squirt, swims around like a tadpole, its tiny brain helping it see and move. As an adult, it attaches to a rock and eats its own eye, main nerve, and brain. It then lives with just a mouth and a stomach!

What do neurons do?

" Neurons are nerve cells that conduct electricity to help you move and feel. Your brain has about 80 billion neurons, all linked together to help you think, move, and perform your body's vital functions. "

" No, because the brain would have no way of getting a blood supply, no nutrition, and no way of connecting to the robot, even with electric wires. But who knows? Maybe it will be possible in a hundred years or so? "

Is it possible to transfer a human brain into a robot?

The moon's gravity tugs on the oceans.

High tide

Low tide

How does the moon affect the tides of the sea?

" **Tides** are caused by the pull of the moon's **gravitational force** on Earth. This pull is greatest on the side of Earth facing the moon. Here, gravity tugs the sea into a bulge, causing a high tide. At the same time, on the opposite side of Earth, where the moon's pull is weaker, the ocean bulges the other way, causing a second high tide. Low tides are caused when the moon's gravitational pull is at its weakest point. As Earth rotates, each ocean on Earth has two high tides and two low tides roughly every 24 hours. **"**

Find out more about the moon on page 89.

High tide

Low tide

Tides

Earth's rotation and the position of the moon make the tides rise and fall. During high tide, the sea comes in and water covers the land. At low tide, the sea goes out and uncovers the land again.

Gravitational force

Gravity is an invisible force between objects. The moon's gravity pulls more strongly on one side of Earth than the other, making the sea bulge as high tides on opposite sides of the planet. Earth's gravity is stronger than the moon's gravity, and this keeps our oceans in place.

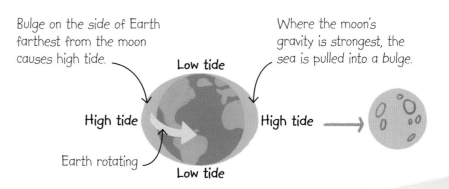

Bulge on the side of Earth farthest from the moon causes high tide.

Where the moon's gravity is strongest, the sea is pulled into a bulge.

Low tide

High tide

High tide

Earth rotating

Low tide

Why doesn't it tickle

❝ When you try to **tickle** yourself, you have to move part of your own body. Your **brain** controls this movement, so it knows you are going to do and feel something. However, when you are tickled by somebody else, there is always an element of surprise or uncertainty that your brain cannot predict. The part of the brain that usually predicts your own movement is called the cerebellum, but it doesn't know what the person sitting next to you is going to do. ❞

Tickle

Some experts think that we became ticklish to improve our self-defense skills—we developed these reflexes (automatic movements) to protect exposed areas of the body. Others think that laughing when tickled helps us bond as humans.

when you tickle yourself?

Motor cortex

The cerebellum helps you control your movements.

Brain

An area toward the front of the brain called the motor cortex controls your voluntary muscles (those under your conscious control). The cerebellum, among other things, helps you balance and makes sure your muscles work together so that you move in a smooth, coordinated way.

Tickle zones

Neck
Armpits
Stomach
Sides
Feet

People can feel ticklish in different places, but these are among the most common areas. Some people start to laugh before they are actually tickled!

How do **birds** fly?

Having thin, hollow bones makes a bird lighter.

Birds have very strong chest muscles, so they can flap their wings and rise.

A bird's body is slim and streamlined, so it cuts easily through the air.

❝ Birds' **wings** are slightly curved on top, but flatter underneath. This means that as a flapping or **gliding** bird moves through the air, the air going over the wing has to travel farther than the air traveling below it. This lowers the air pressure above the wing, creating an upward force called lift that helps in flying. **❞**

Wings

A bird's flapping wings pull it into the sky and thrust it forward. The long, stiff feathers push against the air, providing extra lift and thrust.

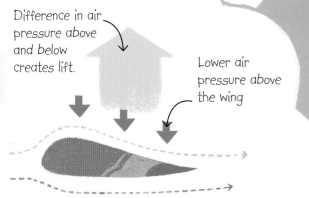

Difference in air pressure above and below creates lift.

Lower air pressure above the wing

Higher air pressure below the wing

Tail feathers help it steer and brake.

Gliding

Long-winged birds can glide great distances, flapping their wings only occasionally. This way of flying saves energy.

Could humans ever fly?

"Humans have always wanted to fly. Since earliest times, people have strapped homemade wings onto their arms and flapped around on hilltops, trying to take off. Yet we are fatter than birds; our bones are not hollow; and we have feeble chest muscles, so jumping off a hill was always likely to be painful. Today, humans can fly... but only because we came up with the clever idea of making aircraft."

Gulls can launch themselves into the air from sheer cliffs.

Eagles often glide upward on rising air currents. This is called soaring.

How do planes go so fast?

Find out how birds fly on pages 82–83.

History of flight

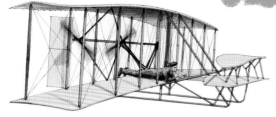

Wright brothers biplane
The Wright Flyer made
the first engine-powered flight
at Kitty Hawk beach in North Carolina
in 1903. The Flyer's first flight was
a short hop of 120 ft (36 m) in
12 seconds.

Curtiss Robin J-1
This propeller-driven aircraft was first flown
in 1928. In 1929 it set an endurance record
by flying for 17 1/2 days. Its angled propeller
blades reduced air pressure in the front of
the airplane, pulling it forward.

X-43A
The record-breaking X-43A
jet reached speeds of
nearly 7,000 mph
(11,300 kph) in 2004.

Drag

Drag is a force that tries to slow planes down. It's caused by friction from the air as the plane flies forward.

Jet engines

When a jet aircraft burns fuel, jets of hot gases shoot out of the back of its engines and thrust the plane forward.

Direction of drag

Streamlined

Fast jets have smooth, pointed shapes so they cut through the air easily and keep drag to a minimum.

" Throughout the **history of flight**, planes have gotten faster and faster. To fly fast, a plane has to overcome **drag** (air resistance), so fast planes are very **streamlined**. The fastest planes have **jet engines**. Jet planes can generate much more power than earlier planes, which had propellers. They can also fly much higher—a propeller can't work very high up in the sky because the air is too thin. The thinner air also means that there is less resistance, making planes even speedier. The fastest jet, the X-43A, flew at an altitude of more than 20 miles (30 km). **"**

The natural oil on the surface of the **skin** is called sebum, which gets washed off in your bath. Then water passes through the skin, and the tissues underneath swell up. Some scientists think this wrinkly effect is a result of evolution. They claim it makes it easier to grip wet things. Our ancestors spent hours **fishing** for underwater food, so maybe wrinkles helped them grab what they wanted to eat. It's a clever idea, but who knows if it is right? When you are in the bath, do wrinkles help you pick up a slippery bar of soap or a rubber duck?

Why does our skin get all

The epidermis is the skin's outer covering.

Glands make oily sebum to coat and protect the skin.

The dermis contains blood vessels, sweat glands, and hair follicles.

Nerve endings detect touch, heat, or pain.

Tiny blood vessels called capillaries lie near the surface.

Skin

The skin is made of two layers, the epidermis and the dermis. The skin protects you and keeps out germs. When we put our fingers in water, the wrinkly effect is increased by nerve fibers in the skin, which narrow, or constrict, fine blood vessels.

Find out more about skin on pages 46-47.

Fishing

Before early people invented rods, nets, and spears, they caught fish with their hands. Some scientists believe that wrinkly fingers would have helped them grab fish more easily, giving them a better chance of surviving.

Fish are slippery and difficult to grasp.

wrinkly in the bath?

Why does the sun seem to follow me everywhere I go?

66 Strictly speaking, the sun doesn't follow us—we follow the sun. That's because Earth is in orbit around the sun. As Earth rotates on its axis, the sun's position in the sky is always changing, but only very slowly. The sun seems to be in the same position whenever we look up, giving the impression that the sun is following us around. 99

Sun

The sun is about 864,940 miles (1,392,000 km) in diameter. You could line up 109 Earths across the face of the sun.

Earth travels 584,018,150 miles (939,886,400 km) in a single orbit of the sun.

Earth rotates on its axis, giving us day and night. This makes the sun appear to move across the sky.

Orbit

Earth travels around, or orbits, the sun, held in place by the sun's gravity. It takes Earth a year to complete one orbit of the sun.

From our position on the ground, we don't usually notice the sun's movement, but we see its effects, such as lengthening shadows.

Why is the moon sometimes out in the day?

" The moon is very luminous because it has a pale surface and because it is very close to Earth. Its orbit around Earth is not a perfect circle and varies a little bit. If the moon is in the right position, it may reflect the sun's rays off its pale surface toward Earth— and that's when we see it in the daytime. **"**

How do you make

> It seems that one of the first nations involved in **making toilet paper** was China. By the 1300s, when China was a great empire ruled by **Emperor Hongwu**, it was made in large quantities. Toilet paper is strong tissue paper made from very fine wood chips. These are ground into flakes and stirred in water until they form a mush called pulp. This is dried and rolled out into long sheets. The resulting paper is soft and has tiny air holes, which help it absorb liquid. "

Making toilet paper

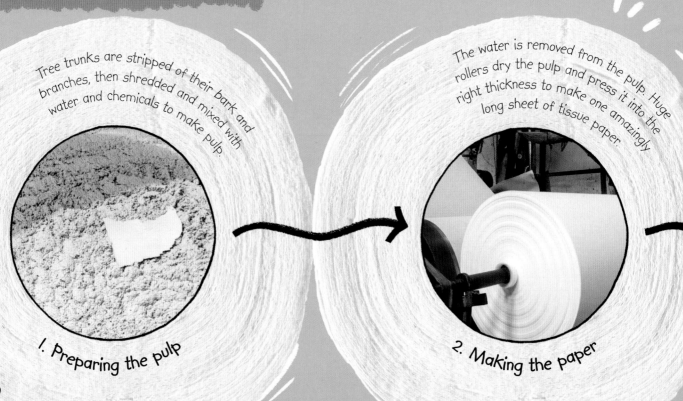

Tree trunks are stripped of their bark and branches, then shredded and mixed with water and chemicals to make pulp.

The water is removed from the pulp. Huge rollers dry the pulp and press it into the right thickness to make one amazingly long sheet of tissue paper.

1. Preparing the pulp

2. Making the paper

toilet paper?

Emperor Hongwu

The Chinese emperor Hongwu (who was born in 1328) and his family are said to have liked their comfort. They used 15,000 sheets of toilet paper a year, each one soft and perfumed. This was an improvement on ancient times. People in the Middle East 2,000 years ago used to use pebbles to wipe themselves. This must have been quite uncomfortable!

Recycled roll

Some toilet paper is made from old newspapers. These are turned back into pulp, cleaned, and made into new toilet paper rolls. Recycling paper like this means that we cut down fewer trees... and that's great for the planet!

Next, the paper is cut into strips, perforated (so you can tear off pieces), and wound onto cardboard tubes to make giant toilet paper rolls! A saw slices these up, cutting them into smaller rolls.

The toilet paper rolls are packaged and sent to stores, where we buy them to use at home.

3. Winding and cutting

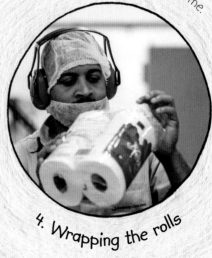

4. Wrapping the rolls

Why do stars twinkle?

Stars

The stars we see are part of a vast family of stars called the Milky Way galaxy. It contains about 200 billion stars.

❝Stars don't actually twinkle. For example, our sun is a star, but because it is so close, it gives a powerful, mostly steady light that comes straight through the **atmosphere** surrounding Earth. Other stars are far away, so their light rays seem more feeble. Our atmosphere is always slightly in motion, so as the light rays from these distant stars hit it, we see a twinkling effect. **❞**

Atmosphere

The atmosphere is like a blanket of gases surrounding Earth. It's made mostly of nitrogen and oxygen. We call this gassy mixture air, and it is constantly on the move.

Strong light from the sun travels straight through the atmosphere.

Distant star

Sun

Weak light from a star is bent and bounced around by moving air, so the star seems to twinkle.

Atmosphere

What's inside your face and head besides your brain?

66 Your head contains your **sense organs**. It also holds your jaws and teeth. Your face includes the muscles that help you smile and show emotions. There are nerves that connect to the brain, called cranial nerves. The brain itself is protected by the fluid and membranes surrounding it. Inside your skull are air-filled spaces that vibrate when you speak or sing and that give you the unique sound of your voice. 99

Optic nerve
The optic nerve sends signals from 125 million light receptors in the eye to the brain's visual cortex.

Ear

Spinal column

Blood vessels

Tongue
The sides, back, and tip of your tongue have more taste buds than the middle.

Epiglottis

Sense organs

Your sense organs are your eyes and ears, and your mouth, nose, and tongue. They contain cells called receptors that tell your brain about the world around you.

> Your tongue and mouth have about 8,000 taste buds. The nerve endings of the taste buds can identify different molecules in the food we eat. We think that taste buds are programed to recognize just five tastes: sweet, salty, sour, bitter, and savory, also called umami.

Why do different foods taste sweet, sour, and bitter?

Skull

Nasal cavity
Scent receptors at the top of the nasal cavity send messages to the brain so it can figure out what you're smelling.

Cells
The cells in your nose and mouth are very sensitive and help you tell the difference between lots of flavors.

Mouth

Teeth

Taste buds

Taste buds are found on folds and bumps on the tongue's surface. Each taste bud is a cluster of taste-detecting receptors.

Why can't we live without trees?

Burning fossil fuels gives off CO_2.

Dead animals and plants release carbon back into the air when they decay.

> " Aside from their beauty, fruits, and valuable wood, trees are also a crucial part of the **carbon cycle**. They take in carbon dioxide from the air and give off oxygen. We wouldn't survive if the air had lots of carbon dioxide in it, so we literally need trees for life. "

Carbon cycle

All living things contain carbon. So do many nonliving things, such as fossil fuels, rocks, and air. Carbon constantly moves between living things, the oceans, the atmosphere, and the land.

Deforestation

Unfortunately, in some parts of the world, people are cutting down forests and using the land for farming. This is called deforestation. If we cut down too many trees, the amount of carbon dioxide in the atmosphere will rise. We need to be much more aware of the value of trees to sustaining life.

Why do trees swallow carbon dioxide?

66 Trees and other green plants use carbon dioxide (CO_2) to make their food—a sugar called glucose. The leaves absorb carbon dioxide, and the tree combines it with water taken in by its roots to make glucose. This process is called **photosynthesis**, and it's powered by sunlight. Oxygen is a waste product of photosynthesis, so the tree releases it into the air. Breathing this oxygen keeps us animals alive. 99

Green plants absorb CO_2 from the air.

Animals eat plants, which contain carbon. They breathe out CO_2.

Energy from sunlight powers the plant.

Find out more about trees on pages 100–101!

The plant releases oxygen into the air.

The plant absorbs carbon dioxide from the air.

The plant absorbs water through its roots.

Photosynthesis

During photosynthesis, leaves use a green substance called chlorophyll to absorb energy from sunlight. Chlorophyll is also the substance that gives leaves their green color.

How do our bodies heal?

66 When you cut yourself, damaged tissue releases chemical messages into your bloodstream. Red blood cells gather to form a **clot** to stop the bleeding, while white blood cells fight any bacteria and infection. New cells grow from the edge of the wound, and cells called fibroblasts enter the **scab** to make strong, fibrous tissue and a substance called collagen, which forms a scar. New blood vessels and nerves grow into the area, and new skin cells complete the healing and replace some collagen. When you are very young, you heal so well that you may not scar at all. 99

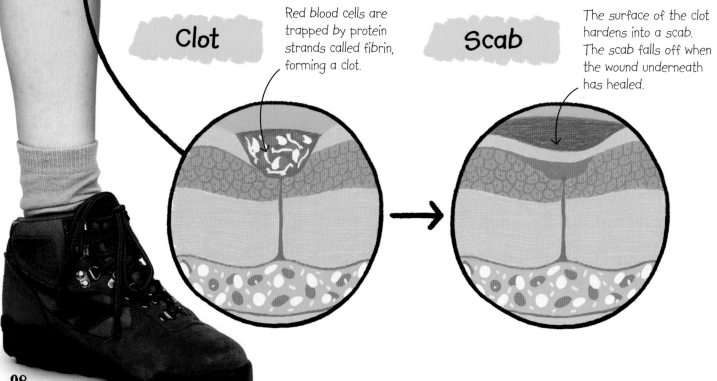

Clot

Red blood cells are trapped by protein strands called fibrin, forming a clot.

Scab

The surface of the clot hardens into a scab. The scab falls off when the wound underneath has healed.

Why do people itch?

66 Skin contains nerve endings that are stimulated when they come into contact with certain things that irritate or inflame the skin. These include dust, insects, allergens, drugs, bugs, and disease. The same nerves that register pain send itchy messages to your brain, which can trigger a response to scratch the area and ease the itching. 99

Scratching tells your nerves to stop sending itchy signals to your brain.

Why do you feel cold with a fever?

66 Your brain has a built-in thermostat that controls temperature called the **hypothalamus.** One of its many jobs is to keep your temperature at 98.6°F (37°C). When your hypothalamus senses that you're too hot, it sends signals to your sweat glands to sweat to cool you. Sweating may make you feel too cold, so you shiver. 99

Hypothalamus

The sugar-cube-sized hypothalamus tries to keep all our body systems in balance so we stay healthy.

When you shiver, it's the hypothalamus trying to keep your body temperature normal.

"**Trees** do not normally shed, or drop, leaves in summer unless their environment is threatened—for example, after a long spell of hot weather with little rain, when there is much less moisture in the soil. Under these difficult conditions, a tree sheds its leaves, entering a period of **dormancy.**

Evergreen conifers often have leaves shaped like needles or scales.

Deciduous trees have large flat leaves.

Trees

There are two main types of tree: deciduous and evergreen. Deciduous trees shed all their leaves in the fall and winter. Evergreen trees, such as most conifers, normally keep their leaves all year round.

Why do some trees lose

Find out more about trees on page 96–97.

Spring
Spring sunshine and rains cause new leaves to burst from buds. Many trees also flower in spring.

Summer
By summer, the tree has lots of leaves to allow it to absorb as much sunlight as possible.

The seasons

The leaves of a deciduous tree sprout in spring, and by summer the tree is thick with green leaves. The leaves capture sunlight and use it

The tree stays like this until rain returns. A similar thing happens if there is heavy flooding with dirty or contaminated water over a long period. Also, trees may lose leaves if they are infected, perhaps with a virus or a fungus, or infested with insects. This can occur throughout the year and may protect the tree from disease and other threats. **"**

leaves in the summer?

Dormancy

Dormancy is similar to hibernation. Just as animals hibernate in winter, plants slow everything down in the winter months to help them survive. Bare trees may look dead, but they're really just resting!

to make food for the tree. In fall, the leaves turn red, orange, and gold before dropping off. In winter, the tree is bare.

Fall
In fall, the days get shorter, and there is less sunshine. The leaves change color and start to drop off.

Winter
In winter, days are the shortest of all, and the soil may be frozen. The tree has now lost all its leaves.

How do volcanoes erupt?

❝ In a few parts of the world, where the Earth's **crust** is thin or cracked, molten rock, called **magma**, is quite close to the surface. Sometimes magma oozes through cracks on the deep ocean floor. At other times, magma and volcanic gas build up until they blast open the rocky surface in a massive explosion. Ash, dust, and gas shoot up to 12.5 miles (20 km) into the atmosphere, and hot magma (now called lava) rains down. Lava may also flow over the land, burning everything in its path. **❞**

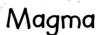

Magma

As rocks are melted by the intense heat inside our planet, gooey magma forms deep underground, in the lower crust and upper mantle.

Crust

The crust is the Earth's hard outer layer. Under this is a softer layer, the mantle. The center of the Earth is called the core.

How do rocks turn into lava?

"Rock never turns directly into lava. Lava is what we call magma when it erupts out of volcanoes. Rocks melt underground to form magma, and it's only when the magma bursts or oozes onto the Earth's surface that we call it lava. Rocks near or at the surface can melt and turn into magma too if they get pushed deep underground by the movement of the huge rocky slabs that make up the Earth's crust."

Geothermal energy

Earth's inner heat is called geothermal energy. Scientists and engineers have discovered how to put it to good use. They drill down to where water trapped underground is heated by magma until it turns into steam. This steam turns turbines that power electricity generators. It's a pollution-free way of making electricity.

Steam from water heated by magma is fed into the power station.

The steam turns turbines in power stations. When the steam cools, it turns back to water, and is pumped back underground.

Glass is **silica**, made from melted sand. Sand has to be heated to very high temperatures before it melts—at around 3,000°F (1,700°C). When it cools, it loses its yellow color. Such high temperatures need a powerful furnace, so it's remarkable that humans first made glass around 5,500 years ago, when it was highly prized for jewelry. Today, glass has many uses, and people make **flat glass** sheets for window panes. 🙶🙶

How exactly is

Glass can be blown into different shapes when molten.

Flat glass

glass for window es is made by melting d, lime, and soda. The ten glass is floated in ath of liquid tin so that rms sheets. Then it's

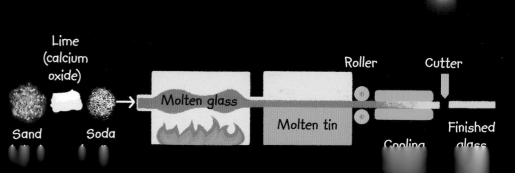

Lime (calcium oxide)

Sand   Soda   Molten glass   Molten tin   Roller   Cutter

Cooling   Finished glass

Why are diamonds so hard?

" Diamond, one of the hardest natural substances, is pure carbon. In a diamond, each carbon atom is closely attached to other carbon atoms and bonded firmly, giving it amazing strength. "

Diamond-tipped dentist's drill.

Each diamond atom forms a pyramid with its four neighbors, making diamond super hard.

glass made?

Sand feels soft because it is made of many fine grains, but each grain is quite hard.

Silica

Silica occurs naturally as sand, and it's also found in many rocks. Silica is also used to make silicon chips for computers.

Carbon

Carbon is interesting because it exists in many different forms. Graphite in pencil lead is pure carbon—it is not actually lead at all. However, unlike diamond, this form of carbon is so soft you can write with it.

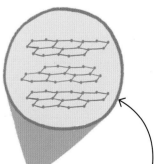

Graphite's carbon atoms are arranged in sheets that slide over each other, so graphite crumbles easily.

We are all born with genes that determine our hair color. The actual color comes from a pigment called melanin, which is made in the hair follicles.

Follicle

A follicle is a tube of tissue surrounding the root of a hair. The follicle is buried in the skin—like a bulb buried in soil.

Hair follicle

Flower bulb

Why does our hair turn

" The root each hair grows from is in a **follicle**. This follicle makes the pigment, or coloring agent, that gives your hair its color. As we **age**, follicles produce less pigment so hair may become gray. Many people are prone to turning gray because of the genes they carry. Some claim a

Find out more about aging on pages 112-113.

Age

How quickly people go gray as they get older depends mainly on their genes. Yet stress, smoking, and illnesses may make it happen faster and at a younger age.

Boo!

gray when we get older?

sudden shock can cause gray hair. So it's probably best not to hide and suddenly shout 'Boo!' at your parents. However, if they are going gray, it's probably because of their genes—which you may have inherited— and has nothing to do with your dreadful behavior! **99**

107

They might, but we don't really know. Astronomers have detected nearly 4,000 **exoplanets** orbiting other stars. Of these, only around 50 or so planets lie in the so-called Goldilocks zone. This means that they orbit far enough away from their stars to not be too hot for life, and close enough to not be too cold. In California, the Search for Extraterrestrial Intelligence (SETI) Institute has scientists working day and night hoping to detect **signals** from alien civilizations. Perhaps we are lucky that we haven't found them, and they haven't found us. "

Golden Record

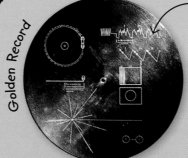

Launched in 1977, the two Voyager spacecraft each carry a disk called a Golden Record of recordings and images to tell aliens about life on Earth.

Signals

We send out signals from Earth in the hope that there could be someone out there. Alien signals might come in the form of radio waves or flashes of laser light.

Do aliens exist?

SETI uses radio telescopes to listen for signals and examine newly found exoplanets.

Exoplanets

Exoplanets are planets beyond our own solar system that orbit, or travel around, sunlike stars. These planets are a very long way away. For example, Kepler-22b is more than 3,640 trillion miles (5,850 trillion km) from Earth.

Kepler-22b

It would take a signal from Kepler-22b nearly 620 years to reach Earth!

"It's unlikely that there is another end to a black hole. A black hole is not a hole in the usual sense of the word. It is better to think of it as an area in space where gravity is so strong that everything pulled into it is massively squeezed into a tiny point. The gravitational force is so great that nothing can escape from the area—even light is permanently trapped by the intense gravity of a black hole."

What is at the other end of a black hole?

Do plants have feelings?

A flower's leaves turn to face the sun so they can collect more sunlight to make food for the plant. Light also warms the flower, making it more attractive to insects.

The *Mimosa pudica* is a member of the pea family.

66 It depends on what you mean by feelings. There is no evidence, I think, of emotions or pain, but plants can sense **light**, with flowers turning toward the sun during the day. The *Mimosa pudica*, which originally came from South America, responds to **touch**. When touched lightly, the plant's leaves fold and droop for several minutes—that's why gardeners like to play with it! **99**

Touch

The *Mimosa pudica's* reaction to touch may fool plant eaters into thinking that the leaves are not good to eat.

Can plants speak?

" No, but they can communicate with each other. When attacked by insects, many plants release molecules into the air or soil. These molecules 'warn' other parts of the plant to defend themselves by releasing special chemicals. Plants growing nearby can intercept these signals and then resist insect attacks using the same chemical response. "

Are there any meat-eating plants?

" Yes. The Venus flytrap, for instance, catches insects in its jawlike leaves. Meat-eating plants like this live in poor soil and get extra nutrition from insects and small animals. In spite of what you may see in movies, I don't think they have ever swallowed a child. "

Why do humans get Old and die?

" All animals age and eventually die. Humans age from the first day of life. At just 48 hours old, nine months before birth, some cells in our bodies start to die. Fortunately, they're replaced by new ones. After birth, this process continues, and eventually cells are not always replaced by new ones—or if they are, the copies are not perfect. The DNA copying process, which makes new cells, gradually wears out. We have much longer lives than most animals, but some fish, whales, and tortoises, for instance, can live even longer. In Bermuda, scientist Dr. Andrea Bodnar has found creatures like sea urchins that live as long as 200 years because their cells do not age like those of humans. "

DNA's twisted-ladder shape is called a double helix.

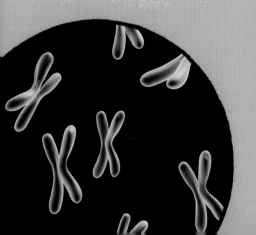

Chromosomes

DNA is found in the nucleus of a cell, coiled up tightly into structures called chromosomes. There are 46 chromosomes in each nucleus, and these form 23 pairs.

DNA

DNA is short for deoxyribonucleic acid. One molecule of DNA has millions of atoms arranged in two spiral strands. DNA is found in all our cells. Our ability to repair DNA decreases as we get older. Damage builds up, causing aging and, eventually, death.

Four different chemicals called *bases* (shown here in different colors) form the "rungs" of the DNA ladder.

Bases give instructions for making proteins—the body's building materials.

Bases are arranged in pairs, and their order forms a code, like letters forming words.

The longest-living land animals are the giant tortoises of the Galápagos Islands. I've met one of these myself—Harriet. She died a few years ago, having met the great scientist Charles Darwin nearly 180 years earlier!

Find out more about aging on pages 106–107.

Why are bubbles round and not any other shape?

" A soap **bubble** is full of air, with a thin film of soapy water surrounding it. The water molecules are attracted to each other, pulling the water into a ball shape. This force of attraction between the water molecules is called surface tension. The force pulls the bubble into the shape with the smallest **surface area** for the amount of air it holds. This shape is always a ball shape, or sphere. "

When you blow a bubble, air gets trapped by a film of soapy water.

Surface area

The surface area is the outside layer of something. These three shapes have the same volume (space inside them), but the sphere has the smallest surface area.

Cube　　Pyramid　　Sphere

Bubble

A bubble is a little like a sandwich. The thin film that surrounds a bubble has two layers of soap with a layer of water in between. Bubbles burst when the water between the two layers evaporates.

Soap

Water

Air

Soap

Water molecules pull together. This surface tension creates the bubble's surface.

Monster bubbles

Adding a liquid called glycerin to your soap solution makes the water evaporate more slowly, giving you stronger, bigger, longer-lasting bubbles. As you wave your bubble wand, the bubbles may start off as long, strange shapes, but they eventually become round.

Bubbles want to be round, no matter what their size!

115

How do you fall asleep?

66 We fall asleep because our bodies are tired and because our brains have rhythms. If you regularly go to bed at 9:00 pm, you are likely to feel sleepy at 10:00 pm, even if you had a nap in the afternoon. This rhythm is controlled by about 50,000 cells—a 'clock' in an area of the brain called the hypothalamus. It is affected mostly by daylight, by when you eat, and by temperature. When we are very young, we need more **sleeping hours.** Ancient people like me need at least five hours. Not getting enough sleep can cause bad health. If you can't sleep, get into a dark, quiet place, wrap up warm, stop worrying, and just let your body relax. **99**

Sleeping hours

The number of hours we need to sleep decreases as we get older. Newborn babies need the most sleep—up to 17 hours a day.

Why do we **dream,** and how do dreams appear in our brain?

❝ We don't really know why we dream. **Dreams** have fascinated, enchanted, saddened, and frightened people since written records began. People have tried to interpret dreams without much success. Some dreams are creative—artists are often inspired by dreams, and some scientists have claimed to be, too. I have brilliant ideas during my dreams but can never remember what they were about afterward. **❞**

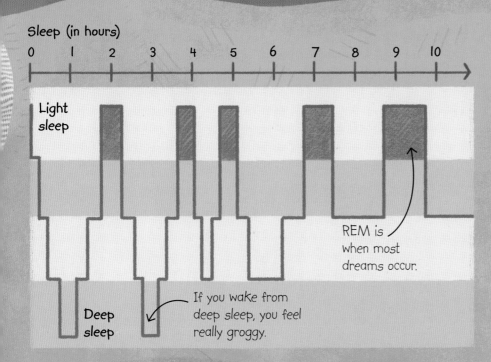

Sleep (in hours)

0   1   2   3   4   5   6   7   8   9   10

Light sleep

Deep sleep

REM is when most dreams occur.

If you wake from deep sleep, you feel really groggy.

Dreams

There are several phases of sleep. The electrical activity in the brain changes during each phase of sleep. Dreams occur at the beginning or often during lighter sleep, just before we wake up. Then our eyes move rapidly. This is called REM sleep (rapid eye movement sleep).

" Our main problem is our dependence on **fossil fuels**. We use these fuels to power our towns and cities, and for transportation. When fossil fuels burn, they produce carbon dioxide. This gas is called a greenhouse gas, because it traps the sun's heat in the atmosphere, sort of like glass trapping heat in a greenhouse. Farm animals make things worse, because they produce methane, another greenhouse gas. "

Why do we Pollute Earth?

Atmosphere

Burning fossil fuels produces carbon dioxide.

Methane comes from farm animals and rotting waste.

Fossil fuels

Coal, oil, and natural gas are fossil fuels, made from the fossilized remains of living things. They formed underground over millions of years.

Greenhouse gases trap heat and warm the planet.

Climate change

Greenhouse gases are heating up Earth. This process is called global warming. It is changing Earth's climate.

Some heat passes through the atmosphere.

118

What are we going to do with all the waste?

❝ We humans are too wasteful. Large amounts of waste are buried or thrown into the sea. More waste could be recycled and the rest turned into energy by burning it. However, burning produces carbon dioxide, so scientists are researching how to capture the carbon dioxide to make burning safer. ❞

It's even been thought that we could blast our garbage into space, but rocket launches would cause even more pollution.

How can we stop pollution?

❝ We could improve things if we took the evidence for **climate change** more seriously. We can start by using renewable energy sources. This means energy from sources that won't run out, such as sunlight, wind, and waves. These energy sources do not produce greenhouse gases. ❞

Wind turbines, like this one, use wind energy to generate electricity. A group of wind turbines is called a wind farm.

Why, when you're doing **boring** things, does time go slowly...

66 When we're standing on planet Earth, time does not change. But I agree, **time** does seem to go slowly when you're bored—and far too fast when you are having fun. This might have something to do with our **perception** of time. If time would only stand still when we are eating an ice pop—but time and temperature make certain that your ice pop melts at a constant rate. 99

Are we almost there yet?

Time

In physics, time is a measurement of how long something takes to happen. It is recorded in seconds, minutes, and hours. Time goes in only one direction, from the past to the present, and then into the future. Time can't be stopped or go backward.

...and why, when you're doing something **fun**, does time go so fast?

Perception

Psychologists are interested in how we experience, or perceive, time. When we're having fun, we're interested in what's going on around us—our brains are active, and we feel that time flies. When we're bored, our brains are less busy, and time seems to drag.

Glossary

abdomen
Also called your "tummy," it contains your digestive system and most major organs

absorb
To soak up or take in

air
Mixture of gases in our atmosphere. It is mostly nitrogen and oxygen, with tiny amounts of carbon dioxide and argon

air pressure
Force of air molecules pressing on objects and surfaces

air resistance
Force that slows down an object moving through air

altitude
Height above ground, usually measured above sea level

astronomer
Scientist who studies the stars, planets, and space

atmosphere
Layer of gases and particles surrounding Earth

atom
Tiny particle of matter. Atoms can bond together to form larger particles called molecules

bacteria
Microscopic single cells living in soil, water, or on the bodies of plants and animals

base
One of four different chemicals forming the "rungs" of a DNA "ladder"

big bang
Idea that the universe began in a huge explosion nearly 14 million years ago

black hole
Region in space with condensed matter where gravity is so strong that no light can escape

bond
Force between atoms or molecules that holds them together

camouflage
Color, markings, movement, or body shape helping animals or plants hide in their surroundings

capillaries
Tiny blood vessels carrying blood to and from cells

carbohydrate
Sweet and starchy foods that are rich in carbohydrates are broken down by the body and are a major source of energy

carbon
Nonmetal atom present in many different molecules, including those in all living things on Earth

carbon cycle
Circulation of carbon from the atmosphere, through living things, and back into the atmosphere

carbon dioxide
Gas made of one atom of carbon and two oxygen atoms, released by animals and taken in by plants

cells
Basic units from which all living things are made

cerebellum
Part of the brain that has many functions, including balance, coordinating movement, and memory

cerebral cortex
Surface layer of the brain's cerebrum, where information is processed

cerebrum
Largest part of the brain, involved with activities such as thought and emotion

characteristics
Features that make us what we are, such as the color of our eyes or hair and how we look and behave

chemical
Any substance made up of atoms and molecules, including any liquid, solid, or gas

chlorophyll
Green chemical used by plants to absorb light for making energy during photosynthesis

chromosome
Tightly coiled strand of DNA in the nucleus of a cell. Chromosomes carry genes

chrysalis
Hard capsule in which a caterpillar changes into a butterfly

collagen
Protein that the body uses to build tissues or to heal wounds

condensation
Change of a gas or vapor into liquid, usually after cooling

core
Earth's hot center, made up mostly of iron and nickel

cornea
Highly sensitive clear layer at the front of the eye

counterweight
Weight that balances another weight

crust
Earth's hard, rocky surface— the planet's outermost layer

dark matter
Invisible matter found in space. It produces gravity, pulling on stars and galaxies

decay
When a dead plant or animal rots (or in physics when an energy source decreases)

dense
When particles in a substance are packed tightly together

dermis
Layer of tissue in the skin below the epidermis

diameter
Distance across a circle, measured across its center

dinosaurs
Extinct reptiles living between 245 and 65 million years ago

dissolved
When a substance mixes completely with a liquid to produce a solution, it is said to have dissolved

DNA
Deoxyribonucleic acid. A chemical that stores genetic information inside living cells

dormancy
Resting stage in a plant's life cycle when active growth slows or stops

double helix
Shape of a DNA molecule with two strands twisted around each other

drag
The force slowing an object down as it moves through a liquid or a gas

electric current
A flow of electricity, consisting of electrons moving through a material

electrical conductor
Any substance through which electricity flows easily

electrical insulator
Material that reduces or stops the flow of electricity

electrical resistance
Measure of how much a material resists the flow of an electric current

electrical signal
Signals in the form of pulses of electricity

electromagnet
Coil of wire wrapped around a piece of iron. When electricity flows through the coil, the iron becomes a magnet

electron
Particle with a negative electric charge that orbits the nucleus of an atom

embryo
Fertilized egg during the first eight weeks of its development that can grow to become a baby

energy
What makes things happen. Light, sound, electricity, heat, and nuclear power are forms of energy. Energy is stored in all matter including food

engineering
Using science and technology to design and build things

epidermis
Outer layer of the skin

equator
Imaginary circle around a planet or moon. It is at the widest diameter, halfway between the North and South Poles

evaporation
When a liquid changes to a vapor

evolution
Development of a species over many generations as it adapts to its environment

exoplanet
Planet beyond the solar system that orbits another star

experiment
Controlled test to see if there is evidence to support a scientific idea

extinct
Plant or animal species that has died out and no longer exists

fat
Major source of energy found in foods and in body tissues

ferromagnetic
Iron-containing material becoming magnetic when placed in a magnetic field

fibroblast
Cell that produces collagen and other fibers

filament
Fine thread or wire. A lightbulb has a metal filament that glows when electricity passes through it

fluid
Substance, usually a liquid, that can flow

fog
Clouds of tiny water droplets that form in the lower atmosphere, often containing particles of dust or smoke

force
Push or pull between objects, which may change their speed, direction, or shape

fossil
Remains or impression of a prehistoric plant or animal, often preserved in rock

fossil fuel
Fuel made from the compressed remains of plants or animals that died millions of years ago, for example, coal

friction
Dragging force reducing movement of an object through contact with something else

galaxy
Vast collection of stars, gas, and dust held together by gravity

gas
State of matter with no shape, because its molecules whiz around freely. A gas will always spread out, given the chance

generator
Device that converts energy into electricity

gene
Inherited part of the DNA that controls a specific function

geothermal energy
Energy harnessed from hot rocks deep underground

gland
Organ or group of cells producing fluids or chemical messages, such as sweat, saliva, or hormones

global warming
Rise in the average temperature of Earth's atmosphere, caused by increasing levels of carbon dioxide and other greenhouse gases

glucose
Type of sugar found in the bloodstream; the body breaks it down to release energy

gravitational pull
Force of gravity between large objects, such as between the Earth and the moon

gravity
Force of attraction that large, dense objects exert, or give off

greenhouse gas
Gas in the atmosphere that traps heat and warms the planet. Greenhouse gases include carbon dioxide and methane

gunpowder
Explosive mixture of the chemicals sulfur, carbon, and potassium nitrate

hair follicle
Group of cells in the skin from which hair grows

halogen
One of a group of very reactive substances. The main halogens are: fluorine, chlorine, bromine, and iodine

hemoglobin
Protein in red blood cells that absorbs oxygen from the lungs, then releases it as blood that is pumped around the body

herbivore
Animal that eats only plants

hibernation
Deep sleep or period of resting of some animals, usually during winter

hormone
Chemical "messenger" traveling in the blood, which controls a particular function

hypothalamus
Part of the brain that links the body's nervous and hormone systems. It keeps the body in a stable condition, so that everything works normally

incandescent
Giving out light as a result of being heated

inert
Unreactive. Inert chemicals do not combine easily with other chemicals

lactic acid
Chemical that builds up in your muscles during tough exercise, when your body breaks glucose down to release energy

lens
Clear rounded structure, which in the eye focuses light on the retina

lift
Upward force produced by a wing as air moves past it

light ray
Light traveling along a straight path

light spectrum
Rainbow colors seen when light is split up into its different colors

liquid
State of matter that flows, taking the shape of its container. A liquid can flow because its molecules slip and slide over each other

luminescent
Ability to produce light

maglev train
Train that uses magnetic forces to float above its track, so that it moves with minimal friction

magma
Gooey, molten rock in Earth's mantle and crust. When it erupts onto the surface, magma is called lava

magnetic field
Force around a magnet that affects other nearby objects

magnetic poles
Two points on a magnet where the magnetic force is strongest, called the magnet's north and south poles

magnifying glass
Handheld lens made of glass or plastic that makes objects appear larger

mammals
Warm-blooded animals with fur or hair that feed their young milk

mantle
Thick, dense layer of rock under Earth's crust. Some of the mantle is partly molten

mass
Amount of matter in an object

matter
Anything that has mass and takes up space—the stuff from which everything in the universe is made

melanin
Brownish pigment found in the skin, hair, and eyes

melanocytes
Cells in the skin producing melanin

melittin
Substance in bee venom that causes pain and irritation when we're stung

membrane
Thin lining around a cell, organ, or other part of the body

meteorite
Piece of rock or metal from space that enters Earth's atmosphere and reaches the ground without burning up

microscope
Optical instrument that enlarges the image of an object using a system of lenses

microscopic
Object that is so small it can often be seen only through a microscope

Milky Way
Galaxy containing our solar system

minerals
Naturally occurring solids in rocks or metals not formed from plant or animal material. Minerals can also mean chemicals that the body uses in food and drinking water

molecule
Particle of matter made of at least two atoms linked by forces called bonds

mucus
Slippery liquid protecting the tubes and cavities in your body, keeping surfaces moist

muscle
Body tissue that contracts to produce movement. Muscles are made up of long cells called muscle fibers

NASA
National Aeronautics and Space Administration, in charge of American space exploration

nerve
Bundle of nerve cells carrying electrical signals through the body

neuron
Another word for a nerve cell

nucleus
Central part of an atom; or in a living cell, the center that controls its functions

nutrition
Process of obtaining food or raw materials (nutrients) needed to stay alive

optic nerve
One of a pair of nerves carrying signals from the retina to the brain

orbit
Path of a body in space, such as a moon around its planet or Earth around the sun

organ
Major structure with a specific function. Organs in the body include the brain, kidneys, liver, and heart

organelle
Part of a cell with a specific function. For example, ribosomes make proteins, and mitochondria generate energy

particle
Tiny speck of matter, such as an atom or molecule. Atoms themselves contain even smaller particles, including electrons, protons, and neutrons

perception
Understanding of the world or people around us gained through our senses

philosopher
Person who uses logical argument to understand the nature of the universe, life's meaning, and how people should behave

pigment
Pigment gives color to a material. For example, melanin gives your hair its color

pituitary gland
Master gland underneath the brain that signals to other glands to release hormones

placenta
Organ in the womb that takes oxygen and nutrients from a mother's blood and passes them into the baby's bloodstream. It is connected to the baby by the umbilical cord

plasma
Very hot, electrically charged state of matter, in which the electrons are freed from their atoms

pollution
Substances, such as those made by factories, cars, and farms, that contaminate the environment

protein
Building blocks of life that are in our cells. Proteins are essential for growth and repair of the body's tissues. Also found in foods such as milk and cheese

psychologist
Scientist who studies human behavior and the workings of the mind

radius
Distance from the center of a circle to its outside edge. It is half the diameter of a circle

receptor
Body in a cell that responds to messages from other cells. Some nerves are receptors that sense changes in our surroundings and send signals to the brain

recycling
Reusing your waste, saving resources and energy

red blood cell
Blood cell that carries oxygen around the body

red giant
Star near the end of its life that has cooled and swelled massively

reflex
Automatic reaction to something affecting the body, such as withdrawing your finger the moment it touches something hot

refract
Bend or change the direction of a light ray as it passes from one material to another, such as from air to water

REM sleep
Period of light sleep when you tend to dream. REM stands for "rapid eye movement." During this stage of sleep, you cannot move, but your eyes flicker

renewable energy
Source of energy that will not run out, such as sunlight, wave power, or wind power

reptile
Cold-blooded animal with a backbone and scaly skin. Most reptiles lay eggs

resists
Works against, or in opposition to, something

respire
Living things respire when using oxygen to release energy from nutrients

retina
Layer of light-sensitive cells inside the back of the eye

scab
Hard crust that forms from a clot and collagen over a wound

sebum
Oily liquid produced by the skin that keeps skin and hair soft and flexible

semiconductor
Material that only conducts electricity under certain environmental conditions, such as temperature

sense organs
Your eyes, ears, nose, and taste buds, and also the skin, which has receptors for touch, temperature, and pain

solar system
Planets and their moons and bodies, such as asteroids and comets, that orbit our sun

solid
State of matter with a relatively fixed shape. Solids don't flow much or change shape like liquids and gases

southern hemisphere
Half of the Earth that lies south of the equator

species
Living things that have very similar genes, look alike, and can breed with each other

spherical
Ball shaped

star
Vast ball of hot, glowing gas in space

static electricity
Positive or negative electric charge on an object's surface produced when it loses or gains electrons. Lightning is an example of static electricity

steam
Gaseous state of water formed when water boils and expands

stereoscopic vision
Single image that our brain forms by combining the two slightly different views from each eye. It enables us to see in three dimensions (3-D)

streamlined
Having a smooth, narrow, often pointed shape to pass easily through air or water. Birds, for example, are streamlined

substance
Particular type of material

sun
Medium-sized star at the center of a solar system

surface area
Size of the entire surface of a shape, often a triangle, square, cube, or sphere

surface tension
Force in the surface of water. It creates a delicate skin that can support tiny objects, such as insects

taste buds
Receptors on your tongue and in your mouth that can identify certain chemicals in the foods you eat

thrust
Force that pushes an aircraft, boat, or vehicle forward. In planes, thrust comes from propellers or jet engines

tissue
Group of similar cells that carries out a function, such as muscle tissue

turbine
Machine that uses a stream of liquid or a gas to turn a generator and produce electricity

umami
Savory taste recognized by your taste buds

umbilical cord
Cord containing blood vessels connecting a baby to the placenta in the mother's womb

universe
All of space and everything that it contains

uterus
Also called the womb, it is the organ in the abdomen where a baby develops before birth

vacuum
Total absence of matter

vaporize
To turn from a solid or liquid into a gas

vapor
Another word for gas, especially a gas evaporating from a liquid that is not hot enough to boil

venom
Poison used by animals to protect themselves against other animals or to injure, paralyze, or kill them

virus
Microscopic, nonliving germ consisting of a package of chemicals. It takes over a cell to make copies of itself and may cause disease

visual cortex
Part at the back of your brain that deals with signals coming from your eyes

water cycle
Nonstop movement of Earth's water between the oceans, sky, and land

water vapor
Water droplets in a gaseous state. It can condense in the air to form clouds

wavelength
Distance between the peak of one wave of energy, such as light or sound, and the peak of the next wave

white dwarf
Small, dense remains of a dying star

wingspan
Distance between the tips of the wings of a bird, insect, or aircraft

Index

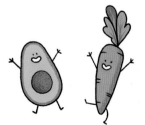

DK | Penguin Random House

Senior Editor Marie Greenwood
Senior Art Editor and Jacket Designer Fiona Macdonald

Senior Editor Phil Hunt
Senior Designer Katie Knutton
Editorial Assistant Katie Lawrence
Design Assistant Xiao Lin
Design Jim Green, Charlotte Jennings, Lucy Sims
US Editor Liz Searcy
US Senior Editor Shannon Beatty
Jacket Coordinator Issy Walsh
Picture Researcher Sakshi Saluja
Managing Editor Laura Gilbert
Managing Art Editor Diane Peyton Jones
Producer, Preproduction Dragana Puvacic
Producer Basia Ossowska
Creative Director Helen Senior
Publishing Director Sarah Larter

Illustrator Alexandra Bye
Photographer Ruth Jenkinson
Contributor Steve Setford
Consultant Lisa Burke

First American Edition, 2019
Published in the United States by DK Publishing
1450 Broadway, Suite 80, New York, NY 10018

Text copyright © Professor Robert Winston 2019
Copyright in the layouts, design, and all other elements
of the Work (including, for the avoidance of doubt, all
text not supplied by the Proprietor) shall be vested
in the Publishers.
Copyright © 2019 Dorling Kindersley Limited
DK, a Division of Penguin Random House LLC
19 20 21 22 23 10 9 8 7 6 5 4 3 2 1
001–314171–Jun/2019

All rights reserved.
Without limiting the rights under the copyright reserved above,
no part of this publication may be reproduced, stored in or
introduced into a retrieval system, or transmitted, in any form,
or by any means (electronic, mechanical, photocopying,
recording, or otherwise), without the prior written
permission of the copyright owner.
Published in Great Britain by Dorling Kindersley Limited

A catalog record for this book is available from the
Library of Congress.
ISBN: 978-1-4654-8444-4
DK books are available at special discounts when purchased
in bulk for sales promotions, premiums, fund-raising, or
educational use. For details, contact: DK Publishing Special
Markets, 1450 Broadway, Suite 801
New York, NY 10018
SpecialSales@dk.com

Printed and bound in China

A WORLD OF IDEAS:
SEE ALL THERE IS TO KNOW

www.dk.com

Acknowledgments

DK would like to thank the following: Caroline Hunt for proofreading; Helen Peters for the index; Nityanand Kumar (DTP Designer) and Seepiya Sahni (Art Editor) for work on cutouts; and Abigail Luscombe for picture research.

Picture credits: (Key: a-above; b-below/bottom; c-center; f-far; l-left; r-right; t-top) **10 Dreamstime.com:** Sebastian Kaulitzki / Eraxion (bl). **11 Science Photo Library:** Edelmann (br). **12 Science Photo Library:** Mark Garlick (t). **13 NASA:** CXC / CfA / M.Markevitch et al (br). **15 123RF.com:** Eric Isselee / isselee (crb, br). **Fotolia:** Anatolii (bc). **16 123RF.com:** Evgenii Zadiraka (cra). **17 Dreamstime.com:** Yekophotostudio (cb). **18 123RF.com:** cherrymerry (cra). **19 Dreamstime.com:** Astrofireball (tr). **20-21 Alamy Stock Photo:** Zoonar GmbH. **21 123RF.com:** Yulia Petrova (r). **22 Dorling Kindersley:** Natural History Museum (bc). **Science Photo Library:** Masato Hattori (ca). **23 Dreamstime.com:** Stevehep (b). **24 Alamy Stock Photo:** RubberBall (br). **Getty Images:** Clarissa Leahy. **26-27 Getty Images:** Jonathan Knowles (c). **27 Dreamstime.com:** gilmanshin (tr). **28-29 Dreamstime.com:** Beijing Hetuchuangyi Images Co, . Ltd . / Eastphoto (t). **30 Dreamstime.com:** Matee Nuserm (cl). **iStockphoto.com:** Mathisa_s (c, cr). **31 Dorling Kindersley:** Jerry Young (cla). **Dreamstime.com:** Alexander Potapov (t); Nancy Tripp / Qnjt (c). **32 Alamy Stock Photo:** Walter Oleksy (l). **34 Alamy Stock Photo:** Nature Picture Library (r); robertharding (l). **35 Dreamstime.com:** Jamiemuny (cr). **iStockphoto.com:** Stocktrek Images (br). **36-37 Dreamstime.com:** Maksim Toome / Mtoome (c). **37 Dorling Kindersley:** Science Museum, London (clb). **Dreamstime.com:** Alexey Romanenko / Romanenkoalexey (ca). **38 Science Photo Library:** DR Keith Wheeler (cb). **38-39 Alamy Stock Photo:** Daniel Sanchez Blasco (bc). **Getty Images:** Clouds Hill Imaging Ltd. (c). **39 Alamy Stock Photo:** Daniel Sanchez Blasco (tl, cra). **Getty Images:** Robert Clark (cr). **Dreamstime.com:** Alle (clb); Rolfgeorg Brenner (bc). **41 Science Photo Library:** Claus Lunau. **46 Getty Images:** A.B. / Lars Langemeier. **48 Dreamstime.com:** Maxim Weise (bl). **49 Alamy Stock Photo:** Teresa Otto (br). **50 iStockphoto.com:** Monica Click. **51 Dreamstime.com:** Lim Seng Kui (tc); Mimagephotography (ca). **iStockphoto.com:** Claudiad (cra). **54-55 Dreamstime.com:** Markus Gann / Magann (t). **56 Alamy Stock Photo:** Roberto Nistri. **57 Science Photo Library:** Dante Fenolio (b). **58-59 Alamy Stock Photo:** DPK-Photo (b). **59 Dreamstime.com:** MRMake (br). **60-61 123RF.com:** Helmut Knab. **61 Dreamstime.com:** Matthias Ziegler / Paulmz (tl). **Fotolia:** Mikael Damkier (tr). **62 Alamy Stock Photo:** Kim Christensen (bc). **63 Dorling Kindersley:** Stephen Oliver (br). **64 Dreamstime.com:** Kdshutterman (l); Milkos (tr). **65 Alamy Stock Photo:** Aaron Amat (br). **66 Dreamstime.com:** Jose Manuel Gelpi Diaz (br). **Getty Images:** Frank Krahmer / Photographer's Choice RF (bc). **69 123RF.com:** olivierl (cla). **Alamy Stock Photo:** Alexandre Watanabe (cr). **70-71 Fotolia:** Sherri Camp (c). **72 Dorling Kindersley:** Andy Crawford (cb). **72-73 ESA / Hubble:** NASA. **74-75 Dreamstime.com:** Mark Turner. **76 Science Photo Library:** Georgette Douwma (bl). **77 Science Photo Library:** KTSDESIGN (tl). **79 Alamy Stock Photo:** Tom Uhlman (t). **82-83 Dorling Kindersley:** Whipsnade Zoo. **83 Dreamstime.com:** Menno67 (bc). **84 Dorling Kindersley:** Planes of Fame Air Museum, Valle, Arizona (cb). **Science Photo Library:** NASA (crb). **84-85 123RF.com:** phive2015. **86 Alamy Stock Photo:** (clb). **86-87 Alamy Stock Photo:** Daniel Sanchez Blasco (b). **Dreamstime.com:** Tatya Luschyk (c). **88-89 Getty Images:** Martin Hartley. **89 Alamy Stock Photo:** Darryl Gill (r). **90 Dreamstime.com:** Hunterbliss (bl); Hxdylzj (br). **91 Getty Images:** Paulo Fridman / Corbis (br); Jeff T. Green (bl). **92-93 Alamy Stock Photo:** Charlie Nowlan. **95 Depositphotos Inc:** gorkemdemir (fbr). **Dreamstime.com:** Tom Wang (br). **96 123RF.com:** grigory_bruev. **Getty Images:** Nelson Luiz Wendel (bl). **97 Science Photo Library:** B.W.Hoffman / AgstockUSA (cb). **99 Alamy Stock Photo:** Mandy Godbehear (bc). **100-101 iStockphoto.com:** urfinguss (c). **102 123RF.com:** Siim Sepp (tr). **104-105 Alamy Stock Photo:** Julian Money-Kyrle. **105 Dreamstime.com:** Pictac (br); Alexander Pladdet (clb). **Science Photo Library:** Dennis Kunkel Microscopy (c / Dental drill bit); Photo Researchers, INC. (c). **106-107 Getty Images:** Indeed (t). **108 Alamy Stock Photo:** J Marshall - Tribaleye Images (c). **Science Photo Library:** DR Seth Shostak (br). **109 NASA:** Ames / JPL-Caltech (cl). **110 123RF.com:** Noppharat Manakul (bl). **112 Alamy Stock Photo:** Science Photo Library (bl). **114-115 123RF.com:** Ilya Akinshin (Bubbles). **114 123RF.com:** Ilya Akinshin (t); pat138241 (bl). **115 Alamy Stock Photo:** Zoonar GmbH (b). **116 iStockphoto.com:** aabejon (crb). **118 123RF.com:** Steve AllenUK (cr). **119 123RF.com:** Alphaspirit (br). **Dreamstime.com:** Whilerests (cl). **120 123RF.com:** Алексей Пацюк (cl). **121 123RF.com:** Narongrit Dantragoon (Background); Hemant Mehta (br).

All other images © Dorling Kindersley
For further information see: www.dkimages.com

The publisher would like to thank the following children for their questions:
Addy, age 9; **Aimee,** age 11; **Akshay,** age 9; **Alfie,** age 9; **Amy,** age 10; **Anika,** age 8; **Archer,** age 8; **Aron,** age 8; **Aubrey,** age 10; **Aurelia,** age 12; **Ava,** age 9; **Ben,** age 8; **Beth,** age 9; **Bonnie,** age 6; **Brayden,** age 7; **Brendan,** age 6; **Camilla,** age 9; **Caroline,** age 8; **Charlie,** age 4; **Charlize,** age 12; **Charlotte,** age 6; **Chase,** age 6; **Chi Yau,** age 11; **Cordelia,** age 11; **David,** age 9; **Devin,** age 7; **Duncan,** age 9; **Eliana,** age 4; **Elijah,** age 15; **Elio,** age 11; **Ellen,** age 9; **Emilia,** age 7; **Emma,** age 7; **Enzo,** age 7; **Eve,** age 11; **Felix,** age 5; **Hannah,** age 6; **Harrison,** age 6; **Him Sum,** age 11; **Ilana,** age 11; **Iris,** age 6; **Isaac,** age 10; **Jackson,** age 8; **Jacob,** age 9; **Jago,** age 8; **James,** age 9; **Jaredin,** age 13; **John,** age 6; **Joseph,** age 7; **Joseph,** age 10; **Kalina,** age 11; **Kate,** age 7; **Kieran,** age 8; **Lia,** age 7; **Liora,** age 6; **Liora,** age 8; **Logan,** age 11; **Louis,** age 11; **Lyra,** age 9; **Mack,** age 6; **Margaret,** age 10; **Mary-Catherine,** age 8; **Melvin,** age 11; **Miriam,** age 7; **Molly,** age 10; **Mya,** age 8; **Naël,** age 11; **Noah,** age 5; **Oliver,** age 7; **Page,** age 16; **Paula,** age 8; **Poppy,** age 10; **Ralph,** age 14; **Rianna,** age 6; **Ruby,** age 11; **Sachin,** age 5; **Segovia,** age 6; **Sophia,** age 14; **Teagan,** age 9; **Theodore,** age 11; **Tzofia,** age 7; **Wakana,** age 6; **William,** age 3; **William,** age 9; **Yi,** age 12; **Elementary school class, California; Primary school class, Cambridgeshire, England.**

Questions submitted from the following countries: Australia, Canada, China, France, Germany, India, Ireland, Japan, Luxembourg, Britain, and the United States.

31901064926670